Never a Dull Moment

Never a Dull Moment

A Libertarian Look at the Sixties

Murray N. Rothbard

Edited by Justin Raimondo

Mises Institute
Auburn, Alabama

Mises Institute
518 West Magnolia Ave.
Auburn, Ala. 36832
mises.org

paperback edition: 978-1-61016-649-2
large print edition: 978-1-61016-650-8
epub: 978-1-61016-651-5

To
Ralph Raico

Contents

Introduction 11

1. Education in California 15
2. Reaching for the Zoning Club 17
3. Desecrating the Flag 19
4. Abolish Slavery! — Part I 21
5. Abolish Slavery! — Part II 23
6. Abolish Slavery! — Part III 25
7. The Middle East Crisis 27
8. We're In a Recession 29
9. Abolish Slavery! — Part IV 31
10. Abolish Slavery! — Part V 33
11. "Little" Israel 35
12. "Rebellion" in Newark 37
13. Abolish Slavery! — Part VI 39
14. Civil War in July, 1967 — Part I 41
15. Civil War in July, 1967 — Part II 43
16. Civil War in July, 1967 — Part III 45
17. The Principle of Secession 47
18. Should There Be a Tax Hike? — Part I 49
19. Should There Be a Tax Hike? — Part II 51
20. Abolish Slavery! — Part VII 53

21. Businessmen for Peace 55
22. "Incitement" to Riot 57
23. Gun Laws 59
24. LBJ — After Four Years 61
25. A New Constitution? 63
26. The Elections 65
27. Why Do They All Hate De Gaulle? 67
28. The Cyprus Question 69
29. How To Get Out of Vietnam 71
30. The Case of John Milton Ratliff 73
31. Jim Garrison, Libertarian 75
32. Whose Violence? 77
33. Devaluation 79
34. Exchange Controls 81
35. The Coming American Fascism 83
36. The *Pueblo* Caper 85
37. The State of the War 87
38. The Garbage Strike 89
39. The Vietnam Crisis 91
40. The Escalation of Lyndon Johnson 93
41. The Amateur "Ideal" 95
42. What Does the Viet Cong Want? 97
43. April Fool Week 99
44. Martin Luther King 101
45. All the Withdrawals 103
46. The Peace Negotiations 105
47. Shooting Looters 107
48. The Revolutionary Mood 109
49. The McCarthy Crusade 111
50. Columbia: Night of Infamy 113
51. The Student Revolution 115
52. Assassinations — Left and Right 117
53. French Revolution — 1968 119

54. Draft Boards 121
55. Humphrey or Nixon: Is There any Difference? 123
56. The New Anarchy 125
57. Nixon-Agnew 127
58. Speaking Truth to Power 129
59. Mao As Free Enterpriser: Or, Halbrook in Wonderland 131
60. Defusing the Baby Bomb 137
61. The New Libertarian Creed 147
62. Confessions of a Right-Wing Liberal 151

Index 163

Introduction

Murray Rothbard was a true polymath. He wasn't just the number one theoretician of the modern libertarian movement — author of the monumental *Man, Economy, and State*; *Conceived in Liberty,* a four-volume history of the American Revolution; the two-volume *An Austrian Perspective on the History of Economic Thought*; and essays too numerous to list — he was also its most tireless publicist, at least in its early days.

He didn't live in an ivory tower: far from it. As he wrote in a 178-page memo entitled "Strategy For Libertarian Social Change":

> If the advancement of liberty requires a movement as well as a body of ideas, it is our contention that the overriding goal of a libertarian movement must be the *victory of liberty* in the real world, the bringing of the ideal into actuality. [Emphasis in original][1]

For Rothbard, libertarianism wasn't an intellectual parlor game, nor was it a personal affectation: for him, it was a banner that was meant to be carried into battle. Ever the happy warrior, he sought to bring the radical libertarian perspective to bear on the events of the day, and it was a task he delighted in. While he tended to write his more serious books and articles in the dead of night, staying up at all hours pounding

[1]"Strategy for Libertarian Social Change," unpublished manuscript, 1978.

away on his old-fashioned (even for the time) typewriter, his "mornings" (noonish) were devoted to relatively lighter fare — the polemical journalism which, over the years, found various outlets. In the 1940s he wrote a personal newsletter, *The Vigil*, which was typewritten and mailed to his closest friends and associates. Later on, he was appointed "Washington Correspondent" for *Christian Economics* magazine, a publication put out by a group known as Spiritual Mobilization, headed up by the Rev. James Fifield, and devoted to economic laissez-faire.

This lasted a few years but eventually he was let go: the right-wing Protestant pastors who were the main audience of *Christian Economics* were appalled by his anti-interventionist polemics when it came to the foreign policy issue. As the cold war got colder there was less tolerance for the "isolationism" of the Old Right, which by that time was largely forgotten by the conservative rank-and-file. Those rightist ministers thought he was a Communist! So there was a parting of the ways.

His sojourn as an occasional writer for William F. Buckley, Jr.'s *National Review* was even briefer, as Rothbard's patience with the warmongering that emanated like a radioactive cloud from that publication soon wore thin. The Buckleyites' crazed desire for a nuclear showdown with Moscow was a bit too much for the old "isolationist" to take, and his refusal to show enthusiasm for World War III soon led to his excommunication from a church to which he had never properly belonged.

But no matter: the hegemony of cold war ideology was about to receive a serious challenge, as the 1960s dawned. An independent libertarian movement — organizationally separate as well as ideologically differentiated from *National Review*-style conservatism — was about to make its debut, in large part due to Rothbard's efforts. He and Leonard Liggio had started *Left & Right*, a magazine directed at the burgeoning New Left movement, which was beginning to make waves, starting on the campus of the University of California at Berkeley. However, the magazine was a quarterly, not a good format for someone who wanted to comment on current events, and so when Robert Lefevre of the Freedom School contacted him to write a syndicated newspaper column for the School's *Pine Tree Features*, Rothbard eagerly took up the task.

These short columns — usually no more than two typewritten pages each — appeared in the Freedom Newspapers, a chain owned by R.C. Hoiles, who was a devotee of Lefevre's and a committed libertarian. Starting in January of 1967, Rothbard churned out fifty-eight columns, the last one written in the summer of 1968, addressing the campus revolt; the massive antiwar demonstrations; the Six-Day War between Israel and the Arab powers; the Newark riots; the Vietnam war; the persecution of H. Rap Brown, the assassination of Martin Luther King, the abdication of Lyndon Baines Johnson, the rise of Richard Nixon — in those two crucial years there was, as they say, never a dull moment.

We might call this Rothbard's "left" period: he sided with the student protestors, the African-Americans fighting cops who had invaded their neighborhoods; he stood with the Vietnamese people against the American soldiers who had invaded *their* neighborhood; he stood with the Palestinians against their Israeli conquerors, he valorized the "heroic" Malcolm X and denounced Martin Luther King for calling for federal troops to put down black "rioters" — but he never pandered to his intended audience. Unlike some of the "left-libertarians" of today, who have adopted the politically correct check-your-privilege jargon of white liberalism, he always addressed the issues in straightforward libertarian terms.

This bluntness is apparent in the very first column, written sometime in January of 1967, cheering the firing of University of California chancellor Clark Kerr, and praising Mario Savio — who had the honesty to say "Good riddance to bad rubbish" — while some New Leftists rushed to defend him. He wondered why conservatives, who had formerly been critics of the educational bureaucracy, didn't side with the student rebels who were rising up against "this educational Moloch" instead of attacking them for "their tastes in clothes and hair styling." Yet the students weren't let off easy, either: instead of protesting Governor Ronald Reagan's threatened cuts to the state university system's budgets, he wrote, they should be cheering and demanding yet *more* cuts because this "acted to reduce the very gigantic university system that the students have properly denounced." So, the New Leftists wanted "self-determination" — or, to put it in the New Age-y terminology of the time, "self-actualization" — as opposed to subservience to a soul-less pedagogical Leviathan? Well, then, "shifting the burden of payment to the student himself will give the student-consumer far more power over their own education" than under the wrong-headed "free tuition" regime.

Rothbard didn't pander: he didn't try to imitate the rhetoric of the students, he didn't insult them by trying to make them think he was "cool": Rothbard was strictly Old School, and never pretended otherwise. What he did was apply libertarian principles to the concrete day-to-day issues that rose up in those two tumultuous years, revealing the radical evil of the State and the unadorned radicalism of the libertarian stance in every case.

He didn't pretend to be a leftist: the idea was to win over the left-leaning students, and the revolutionary blacks, to libertarianism, not to masquerade in the fashionable rhetoric of the moment. He never disguised or watered down his libertarianism to suit his audience: unlike the self-styled "left-libertarians" of today, he rejected any modification or "addition" to the central axiom of libertarian political theory, which is the nonaggression principle plain and simple. In answer to the "check your privilege" sloganeering of the cultural left, Rothbard would have said "Check your cultural prejudices at the door."

Although himself a traditionalist, Rothbard always maintained that there could be no such thing as a "libertarian" culture: those who wanted to "live liberty" were living under a delusion, namely the entirely false idea that some particular "lifestyle" could be derived from the central axioms of what is only a political philosophy and not a "way of life." He had, after all, been badly burned by the cultural totalitarianism of the "Objectivist" cult around novelist Ayn Rand, which had a "party line" on every subject under the sun, including music (Rachmaninoff good, Mozart bad) and even physics. The libertarian movement, or at least a substantial portion of it, had been down that road before, and found it to be a dead end.

To the younger readers of this volume, Rothbard's writings from the 1960s may seem like a recounting of ancient history, and only tangentially relevant to the world we live in today. That this is not so is underscored by one of his more prescient pieces: in "The Coming American Fascism" Rothbard comments on various acts of retaliation against critics of the Vietnam war and writes: "At home we have the fascist corporate state economy: an economy of monopolies, subsidies, privileges runs by a tripartite coalition of Big Business, Big Unions, and Big Government." While "[i]n foreign affairs we have expanded all over the globe, grabbing bases and running governments everywhere, all in the name of a global crusade against the 'international Communist conspiracy.'"

Substitute "international terrorist conspiracy" for that last phrase and we have a snapshot of the future — the one we are living in today.

The material herein is presented in chronological order and is published exactly as written: my insertions are in brackets. The two final essays provide the vital context for the preceding material, explaining Rothbard's break with the conservatives and prefiguring the rise of libertarianism as an independent movement — a development for which he was largely responsible.

— Justin Raimondo

CHAPTER 1

Education in California

Consistency has long been one of the most glaring causalities of our political life; but the typical views on the mess in higher education have been hopelessly muddled even by contemporary standards. Thus, for years conservatives have been attacking the huge and swollen bureaucracies engaged in dispensing higher education, especially the gigantic and ever burgeoning state universities.

Then, two or three years ago, a profound and widespread rebellion against this educational Moloch emerged and accelerated among the students trapped in these universities. Yet, far from embracing these natural allies on the "New Left," the conservatives reacted in horror, called for stamping out the upsurge of youth whom they found to violate their tastes in clothes and hair styling.

For their part, the New Left kids have proven to be almost as self-contradictory. For years they have instructed us all on the impersonal and subtly dictatorial factories these groves of academe have become: and for years Clark Kerr, president of one of the mightiest behemoths of them all, the University of California, has been held up as the most dangerous theoretician of this new and collectivistic "multiuniversity."

But now that Kerr has been fired from his post, the New Left, with the honorable exception of Mario Savio, has leaped to his defense instead of breaking out with cheers of rejoicing.

Furthermore, the New Left has not realized that Governor Reagan, by moving to cut the university's swollen budget has acted to reduce the very gigantic university system that the students have properly denounced. And the New Left, in protesting against Reagan's proposal for charging tuition, has failed to understand that there is nothing progressive about forcing the taxpayers to pay for someone else's education. On the contrary, shifting the burden of payment to the student himself will give the student-consumers far more power over their own education, and ultimately over their own fate.

CHAPTER 2

Reaching for the Zoning Club

There is nothing more important for those who think they believe in freedom, in free enterprise and in private property, than bringing these high-flown generalities to bear on the concrete problems of their daily lives. It is very easy to say, or believe, that one is devoted to freedom, so long as freedom remains a lofty and unanalyzed generality. There is nothing, of course, wrong with such generalities; on the contrary, they are indispensable for any thought or action on this vital subject. But, to be effective or meaningful, they must not remain on the level of generalities; they must brought down and applied, consistently and with determination, to our daily lives.

Take, for one among an infinite number of examples, our zoning laws. The vast majority of people who support and vote for zoning laws undoubtedly think themselves to be staunch adherents to the concepts of free enterprise and private property, while actually their support is one of the most important tools in undermining these very principles.

Here is a man, Mr. Smith, living on a certain lot in a $20,000 house. He then finds that Mr. Jones has purchased the vacant lot next door and intends to build a $10,000 house on the property — or, worse, yet, aims to move in a trailer (or "mobile home") in which to live. Smith becomes highly agitated; he fears that a far cheaper house next door will lower the market value of his own property, or perhaps he is esthetically repelled at the sight of a mobile home. What, then, does he typically do in our gloriously free society? He goes to his local town council and has them pass an ordinance forbidding anyone to build a house worth less than $20,000 on the property — in short, he has turned to that club of tyranny known as the zoning law. He has ruthlessly trampled on the freedom of enterprise and on the property right of his neighbor.

What else could Smith do, one might ask, to maintain the value of his property or the esthetic qualities of the lot next door? The answer is really quite simple. In a truly free society, he would buy the lot next door himself, or, as an alternative, pay Jones, if the latter is willing, the costs of putting up a more expensive dwelling. In short, in a truly free society, each man must pay for what he wants to achieve; he must not load the burden of getting what he wants on to the next man by use of the club and bayonet of organized government.

CHAPTER 3

Desecrating the Flag

Hysteria is sweeping the land about the supposed honor of the American flag, and throughout the country, state, and federal legislators are competing with each other in proposing ever stiffer punishments for the high crime of desecration. Eager-eyed snoopers ferret out any use of flag cloth for covering or in the theater, and the long arm of the law quickly reaches out to apprehend and chastise these often unwitting criminals. We await some fervent patriot proposing death by torture for the high crime of mistreating a piece of cloth with red and white stripes.

For, if we sit back for a moment and reflect on the whole issue, the first thing that should be clear is that this is what the flag is: a simple piece of cloth with parallel stripes of certain colors. And the first thing we should ask ourselves is: What is there about a piece of cloth that suddenly makes it sacred, holy, and above defilement when red and white stripes are woven into it? Contrary to many hysterical politicians, the flag is *not* our country, and it is *not* the freedom of the individual. The flag is simply a piece of cloth. Period. Therefore, he who tampers with or desecrates that piece of cloth is *not* posing a grave threat to our freedoms or to our way of life.

Consider the implications of taking the opposite position: if the flag is *not* just a piece of cloth, this means that some form of mystical transubstantiation takes place, and that weaving a piece of cloth in a certain manner suddenly invests it with great sanctity. Most people who revere the flag in this way are religious; but to apply to a secular object this kind of adoration is nothing more nor less than idolatry. Religious people should be on their guard always against the worship of grave images, and their worship of State flags is just that kind of idolatry.

If, indeed, the flag is a symbol of anything throughout history, it has been the battle standard of the State, the banner it raises when it goes into battle to kill, burn, and maim innocent people of some other country. All flags are soaked in innocent blood, and to revere these particular kinds of cloth becomes not only idolatry, but grotesque idolatry at that, for anyone who loves individual liberty.

There is another crucial point in this whole controversy that nobody seems to have mentioned. When someone buys flag cloth, this cloth is his private property, to do with as he wishes ... to revere, to place in his closet ... or to desecrate. How can anyone believe otherwise who believes in the right of private property? Anti-desecration laws and ordinances are outrageous invasions of the right of private property, and on this ground alone they should be repealed forthwith.

CHAPTER 4

Abolish Slavery! Part I

Any current drive for the abolition of slavery would only draw apathetic shrugs from the American public. Wasn't slavery abolished in the United States over a century ago, and aren't the only remaining signs of it confined to such backward countries as Yemen and Saudi Arabia? The answer is emphatically, No! and we shall be devoting a series of columns to pointing out the vast amount of slavery that still exists — unheeded and accepted — in the good old US of A. As in all cases of slavery, they cry out for abolition, but so far few if any voices have been raised to take up that noble cry.

The outstanding example of slavery still existing in the United States is, of course, the draft. A century ago Americans added the 13th Amendment to the Constitution, which abolished involuntary servitude. If the draft isn't involuntary servitude, it is hard to know how that term can be defined, and yet no part of the American judicial system has bothered to bring the servitude of conscription under the rubric of the Thirteenth Amendment.

Almost everyone admits that the current operations of the draft system are absurd and inequitable, in which some young men are grabbed while other go permanently free. To correct this kind of inequity of oppression, there are two directions in which we can move: draft everyone, or abolish the draft altogether. This idea that if some are drafted then all should feel the yoke is tantamount to saying, in the days of Negro slavery, (a) that if one slave manages to run away, he should be dragged back to slavery in order to be "fair" to his fellow victims, and (b) that everyone in the society should be enslaved equally. The libertarian, in contrast, wants everyone to be free of either the draft or old-style slavery, but he cheers when anyone is able to escape the monstrous yoke. The "draft-everyone" school of egalitarians, furthermore, can never succeed in their aim of imposing compulsory uniformity on all. Because even if everyone is drafted for "national service," a state that Secretaries [Robert S.] McNamara and [W. Willard] Wirtz may be aiming for, only a small number will be sent to the front lines of military service; others will have to grow food, produce equipment, man the supply lines, etc. So any attempt to impose equality of condition violates the nature of the world and must fail.

The rational course, therefore, is to cheer when anyone escapes the draft and to call for its abolition, not to try to make everyone suffer "equally." The only equality that can be achieved in the world, hence the only rational concept of equality, is equality in liberty.

CHAPTER 5

Abolish Slavery! Part II

One common argument in favor of conscription-slavery is that everyone has an "equal obligation to serve" the U.S. government. But apart from the dubious morality of forcing everyone to suffer as much as everyone else, this equality of obligation is impossible to achieve, because not everyone can have equal time in the front lines. Only a few can be in the front lines, to say nothing of cripples, the physically handicapped, etc.

Another common argument for the draft is that this degree of compulsion is necessary for "defense." But then the question arises: defense of whom? Logically, this can be either the defense of the drafted person himself, *or* the defense of other people. In short, we can conscript A either to defend himself, or to defend B, C, D, etc.

The idea that A should be drafted because it is necessary for his own defense is a rather peculiar one. If Mr. Jones needs to be in the army in order to defend himself, then one would think that he should be permitted to decide this for himself voluntarily, and would leap at the glorious chance offered to him. If he really needs to be in the army in order to defend himself, then he will see this and make the choice on his own; there is no need for the State to employ coercion to make him do it. Besides, the idea that adults should be forced to do things "for their own good" is a completely totalitarian one. It is good, let us say, for Mr. Jones to have X number of vitamins per day. Does that mean that he should be forced by law to consume this amount, and that a vast Gestapo of law enforcers be hired to see to it that de does not flout the majesty of the law?

Furthermore, enslavement is a peculiar kind of "defense" against some foe's hypothetical future aggression against Mr. Jones. We may well ask: what kind of aggression would this mistily far-off "enemy" commit against Jones that would be worse, or nearly as bad as, being enslaved into an army in which he might well kill and be killed?

Nothing that any future and dimly seen enemy will do to him is likely to be as vicious as the action committed against him by "his" government, here and now. A curious kind of defense indeed!

And who, we may ask, is around now to defend Jones against the people who are aggressing against him to the point of enslaving him into a military machine? Who is there to defend the draftee against his self-proclaimed "defenders"?

For centuries governments have been trumpeting far-off bogeys as an excuse for enslaving and sending to their deaths people who could be no worse off if the bogey ever really materialized. It is about time that we call a halt. It is about time that we stop our rulers from using this kind of con game to justify slavery and murder on a massive scale.

CHAPTER 6

Abolish Slavery! Part III

Some of those who argue for conscription-slavery concede that it would be wrong to draft someone so that he might defend *himself* against some remote Enemy. But, they add, conscription is needed so that Society might be defended against the foreign enemy. But first we must realize that, as the late great individualist Frank Chodorov once put it, "Society are people." "Society" is, simply, every person except *you*. By what right, then, do A, B, C, and D, put their heads together to decide that E must be enslaved to fight for *their* defense? Surely this is a monstrous moral doctrine. If A, B, C, etc., really feel threatened by some outside invader, then let them take the steps to finance out of their own pockets the military defense supposedly needed to combat that threat; and let *them* either fight in their own defense or hire someone who is willing to do this for them.

There is ample precedent for this: companies and institutions hire guards and night watchmen, millionaires hire bodyguards, etc. So let our fearful patriots either join up themselves or hire people to defend them. Why must the rest of us who either think the Foreign Threat is a lot of nonsense or who consider the alleged defense as bad as the disease, be forced to pay for the protection of those who want it? You and I are not forced to pay for the guards and night watchmen of those who hire them; neither should we be forced to pay for the defense of others on a national scale. And all the more should we not be allowed to enslave unwilling young men and to pay them traditional slave wages for the privilege of defending us, or to wage a war in which they do not believe or to which they are opposed. Let those who feel threatened defend themselves or hire willing men for their defense. Any other set-up is enslavement and confiscation of private property for the benefit of others, i.e., is large-scale robbery.

Some libertarian inclined students at the University of Chicago have recently launched the Council for a Volunteer Military, dedicated to abolishing conscription, and they have managed to enlist supporters from all over the ideological spectrum, from Norman Thomas and James Farmer on the Left, to Karl Hess, Barry Goldwater's speech writer, and Professor Milton Friedman. But, in an effort to achieve respectability, they have made their arguments almost purely technical and pragmatic: that the costs of a volunteer army would not be very great, that continual training of new recruits is costly and inefficient, etc. While the Council recognizes the injustice of enslaving a few men at low wages and thus "taxing" them more than the rest of the citizenry, their emphasis on technical and pragmatic economics misses the really crucial point. The problem is not the inefficiency of a conscript army; the problem is the gross immorality — indeed, the massive criminality — of drafting young men to be kicked around for years of their lives, and then to kill or be killed against their will. If this fundamental moral consideration is not "respectable" these days, then so much the worse for respectability. In true pragmatic fashion, moreover, the Council for a Volunteer Military concedes the wisdom of universal military training as an emergency reserve. With this kind of temporizing, draft-slavery will never be abolished. To achieve abolition the monstrousness of conscription must be sung out, loud and clear and unabashed.

CHAPTER 7

The Middle East Crisis

We cannot fully understand the nature of the crisis in the Middle East by just following today's and yesterday's headlines. There are far deeper and longer lasting factors at work than merely who commands the Strait of Tiran or who is responsible for the latest border skirmish in the Gaza Strip. The first thing that we as Americans should be concerned about is the absurdity of the fundamental foreign policy position of the U.S. government. This is a doctrine that the United States first adopted, to its woe, in the late 1930s and has clung to ever since: the doctrine of "collective security." The collective security thesis assumes that, at whatever moment of time one happens to be in, the territorial distribution of States on the world's surface is just and proper. Any forcible disturbances of any governmental boundary anywhere, then, automatically becomes "aggression" which must be combated either by all other nations or by the United States itself, acting as "world policeman."

In short, the whole thesis of collective security that has guided American policy for thirty years rests on a ridiculous analogy from private property and the function of police in defending that property. Mr. Jones owns the property; it is then certainly not absurd to say that he has an absolute moral right to that property and that, therefore, any invasion of that property by force is immoral and unjust. It is also not absurd, then, to say that it is just for Mr. Jones's property to be defended by some form of police (whether public or private is not here at issue).

But surely it is worse than absurd to leap from this concept of just private property to say that a *State's* territory is equally just, proper, and sacrosanct, and that therefore any invasion of that State's self-acclaimed territory is just as wicked as invasion of private property and deserves to be defended by some form of "police." All State territory, without exception in history or in any part of the world, was obtained, not by legitimate voluntary productive means such as used by Mr. Jones or his ancestors, but by coercion and violent conquest. Therefore no one allocation of territory — certainly no allocation of territory that happens to exist at any moment of time — is *ipso facto* proper and just and deserving of any form of defense. If, in Year 1, Ruritania grabs part of the territory of Waldonia by force, then surely it is nonsensical for the United Sates or some other group to step in with righteous indignation when, in Year 5, Waldonia tries to grab that territory back. Yet this is precisely what is implied in the whole theory on which the United Nations is grounded, and in the U.S. foreign policy to "guarantee the territorial integrity of all the nations in the Middle East."

Basic to the current crisis in the Middle East is the fact that such Israeli territory as the port of Elath, and indeed the entire Negev desert area surrounding Elath, which is now a big bone of contention between Israel and the Arab powers, was grabbed by force from the Arabs by Israel in 1948. For the US, then, to go to war to "defend the territorial integrity" of Israel in the Negev would be, on this and on many other grounds, the height of folly.

CHAPTER 8

We're In a Recession!

We live in a land of euphemism, of changing labels so as to prettify or whitewash the harsh features of reality. And so, undertakers have become morticians, real estate agents have become realtors, press agents have turned into public relations counsel, and even rat catchers have been transformed into exterminating engineers. So has it been with the harsh features of our economic reality.

Down to the late 1930s, when the economy turned downward and economic activity slackened, all economists called such periods *depressions* — and the public knew that, whether the periods of contraction be mild or severe, they were *depressions*. Period. But then, when the patent medicine nostrums peddled by the New Deal to end the depression of the early 1930s led only to another severe crisis in 1937, the Brain Trusters of the New Deal decided that if they could not fix up reality, they could at least juggle its labels. And so *depression* miraculously became *recession*. Depressions were henceforth banished from the land, never to return — by definition. From now on, every economic contraction was to be called by the much milder name of *recession*.

The result was that while depressions were magically banished, we began to suffer a whole series of recessions, dips that seemed suspiciously like the obsolete depressions: in 1948, 1953, 1957, and 1960. After the lengthy boom from 1961 to 1966, one of the longest in American history, our economic managers began to trumpet the idea that recessions, as well as depressions, were a thing of the past, victims of the "fine tuning" management of the wizard regulators and controllers of the New Economics. What a shock, then, when the economy began inexorably to dip and contract again toward the end of 1966! Was reality again about to destroy the cherished vaunting of the nation's Brain Trusters?

But no! Lo and behold! Euphemism and name-juggling came once again to the rescue. *Recession*, too, appears to have been banished by definition. Our economic pundits could not deny that their own statistics revealed a considerable downturn in the economy: in housing and construction, in corporate profits, in capital good investments and industrial production — in short, in all the accepted indicators of what is happening in the economy. But this contraction has not, heaven forbid, been called by the term "recession," which is now too harsh for American consumption. We have suffered, since late 1966, from a "rolling readjustment," a "sidewise movement," or "a pause" — depending on which expert you read. But don't let them kid you: we're in a solid, old-fashioned *recession* — if not depression — though obviously not a particularly severe one. It is possible that when, as seems likely, we pull out of the recession toward the end of this year, the nation's economists and managers will admit that we *were* in a recession — but that *now* things are fine and getting ever better. Or, it's even more likely that the word recession will be quietly buried forevermore. So now we have to worry about "pauses" or "readjustments."

The best way to beat this flim-flam is in the spirit of the angry boy in the old *New Yorker* cartoon: The mother pleads with the boy: "Eat your broccoli, dear." To which the lad replies: "I say it's spinach, and I say to hell with it!"

CHAPTER 9

Abolish Slavery! Part IV

Conscription is quite obviously the most blatant example of slavery in American life, and happily many voices from both Left and Right are now being raised to call for abolition of this unmitigated despoiler of liberty. But there are other critical and pervasive examples of slavery on the American scene that have, for some reason, gone unnoticed even among dedicated libertarians.

One vital example is the armed forces itself. For even a volunteer army practices slavery on a grand scale! It is true that a volunteer army draws its recruits by free choice of the men who enlist. But what happens after they enlist? Suppose that a man enlists in the army for five years. Suppose that after two years he becomes fed up with the regimentation of military life and decides to quit for a better job? Can he do so? Certainly not! In every other occupation in society, a man may quit his job whenever he wants to, and either take another job or quit working altogether. Surely this right is fundamental to a free society; without the right to quit, a man is a slave, even if he originally took the job purely voluntarily. But an enlistee in the armed forces is not allowed to quit before his term expires. If he tries to, he is court-martialed and jailed under harsh military law. This is forced labor and involuntary servitude, however one looks at it.

There are other occupations, too, where a man may sign a contract to work for a term of years; he may, for example, sign on for five years as a geologist to work in Arabia. But he is allowed to quit; he may be considered a moral leper if he thus breaks his contract, he may be blacklisted by other firms hiring geologists, but he is not incarcerated for doing so.

Contrast, then, the armed forces with a very similar kind of occupation: the local police force. A man is free to quit the police force any time he wishes; why then should he not be free to quit the army as well? The armed forces will be centers of slavery not only so long as the draft exists, but even further, so long as a man is forced to stay in the army for any length of time after he decides he would rather call it a day.

No man is free if he does not have the right to quit his job. No one denies this right in every occupation — but one: in the armed forces, where this quitting is called "desertion" and met with imprisonment or even the firing squad.

If we would call ourselves a free country, this system must be abolished.

CHAPTER 10

Abolish Slavery! Part V

The draft — and the military — are the most obvious and blatant examples of slavery in American life today. But there are others — and these areas suffer a great deal more neglect. One all-pervasive example of slavery in present-day America is the enslavement of our children, known as *compulsory attendance laws.* Compulsory attendance laws mean that up to a certain age — sometimes sixteen, sometimes eighteen — our entire population of children is forced into a penned enclosure, often more or less devoid of true education, known as a "school." Most often, furthermore, this is a "public" (or governmental) school.

Now schooling may be a great thing but, like many other good things, it is *not* great for everyone. Many people have neither the inclination nor the ability for schooling, and many of them would be far better off spending these eager and formative years working in a job of their choice, than in spending them miserable, resigned, or embittered, in a supposedly benevolent house of detention known as a public school. Why is there so much juvenile delinquency these days? Well, at the risk of oversimplifying, wouldn't *you* tend to become delinquent if *you* were penned up in a school by force of governmental bayonet, in a place for which you had neither the ability nor the inclination?

America grew great in a society where very few men went to high school, let alone college, and where many workers and businessmen developed and prospered on the job, and without wasting many years trying to become scholars, a task for which they were not suited. It is absurd to think that everyone needs or should get a college education, and it is unfortunate that many businessmen have been brainwashed by this generally held myth so that almost any job above the status of ditch digger these days requires a high school, or even a college, diploma. Worst of all, millions of youngsters have had their spirits broken, and their careers thwarted or shattered, by means of this coerced channeling into the world of schooling and scholarship.

It is often believed that, in this modern world of advancing technology, lengthy school attendance has become necessary. Actually, this is not true at all. Recent studies and experiments have shown that school drop-outs, after not learning anything in eight or ten years of compulsory schooling, have, in a few short weeks, been able to learn enough from private industrial training to take jobs successfully in industry.

There is *one* shrewd method to this madness: the more kids artificially kept out of the labor market, the more the government "deals with" the unemployment problem, and the more people are kept off the labor force who would otherwise compete with, and crack, the artificially high structure of minimum wage laws and union-imposed wage rates. Hence, the labor unions — who, for similar reasons, impose absurdly long periods of apprenticeship training, for low wages, upon their fledgling members — have been the most eager to keep the youngsters out of the labor force by use of the State bayonet. As the eminent Paul Goodman has written in his brilliant work, "Compulsory Mis-education," "Twist it and turn it as you will, there is no logic to the proposal to extend compulsory schooling *except* as a device to keep the unemployed off the streets by putting them into concentration camps called school."

Fortunately, in recent years, writers and sociologists like Goodman and Edgar Z. Friedenberg have turned a caustic light on our system of compulsory schooling; for the first time in many decades, this mischievous system is coming under careful and critical scrutiny.

CHAPTER 11

"*Little*" *Israel*

Why the wave of adulation and admiration that greeted the *blitzkrieg* war of conquest by Israel against the Arab countries? That greeted the conquest, that is, in the United States; most of the rest of the world was stunned and appalled. Has a sickness eaten its way deep into the American soul? Do we all simply love a winner — even if he wins by means of fire-power, surprise attack, and mobile *blitzkrieg* tactics? Even if he wins, as Israel did, by napalming innocent women and children in Arab villages? Have we lost all sense of moral principle, all sense of justice?

Two major reasons have been advanced for the acclaim heaped by American public opinion on the state of Israel. One is that it is a "bastion of anti-Communism in the Middle East." This is an odd argument, since, in the first place, none of the Arab countries is Communist or anything like it; all are governed by deeply religious Moslems. Sure, the Arabs accepted military aid from Soviet Russia, but only after they found that they could not get such aid from the U.S., which was arming Israel instead. And, furthermore, the Arab countries are certainly no *more* socialist than Israel: Israel has been governed, since its inception, by an avowedly socialist party (the Mapai); it has a very large proportion of its economy in government hands; and it has a fantastically strong labor union movement (the Histadrut) which, as a virtual State within a State, controls and owns a large chunk of the economy of Israel in its own right. And, what is more, there exist in Israel the famous kibbutzim, which are communes, in which communism (in its true sense of virtual absence of private property) is practiced on a scale far more intense than in any Communist country in the world (with the exception of China). And while membership in the kibbutzim is generally voluntary, there are also many Israeli refugees literally enslaved to the kibbutzim, and who cannot leave them until they "pay back" the Israel government the passage money from Europe to Israel. Furthermore, since their pay in the kibbutzim is very low, it is almost impossible for them to work out their term, and so they remain, often with great reluctance, in forced labor on the Israel communes.

The other common argument is that Israel is "little," compared to its Arab neighbors, and therefore deserves admiration as an underdog surrounded by giants, as Davids surrounded by Goliaths. The "littleness" here is a complete misreading of world affairs; it would be just as absurd to hail Britain when she conquered India quite easily. Are we to consider the British Empire as the "underdog," since India's population outnumbered England by a huge multiple? Certainly not: clearly the technological level and relative standards of living were so disparate, that the "smaller" nation could easily conquer and dominate the larger. The same is true for "little" Israel. The rulers of Israel are not Middle Eastern, like their Arab neighbors; they are largely European, and furthermore, they are financed very heavily by wealthy European and American Zionists. These, then, were Europeans who came, on the backs of and in collusion with, the British Empire (from the end of World War I to the end of World War II), with European technology, wealth and know-how, to seize the lands and homes of Arabs, and themselves to colonize Palestine. To think of these Zionists and Israelis as "underdogs," in the light of the true situation, is nothing less than grotesque — as can be seen by the swift wars of conquest fought by Israel in 1948, 1956, and now today.

CHAPTER 12

"Rebellion" at Newark

When we hear about Newark — or Watts, or Buffalo, or the other Negro insurrections of the past few years — the first thing we need to do is to gain and keep some perspective on these shattering events. One important point to remember is that the overwhelming majority of the dead and wounded from these conflicts have been Negro — and most of them shot by the National Guardsmen who are so quick to move into the trouble areas. In short, the most important lesson to be learned from Newark or Watts is that we Americans fool ourselves when we think of ourselves as living under a "free government," when we think of our government as operating by some sort of voluntary consent. Ordinarily, when things are going well and there is little to disrupt the permanent reign of the State, we don't *see* the violence, coercion, and terror at the root of the very existence and operation of all of our governments, federal, state, and local. But let any trouble arise to mar the peaceful workings of this coercive rule, and the State reverts — ever so quickly — to its true role: that of naked, organized violence.

Notice how rapidly and how eagerly the State mobilizes its National Guard at the first sign of any danger to one of its violence-wielding units: the local police. Notice how rapidly the State turns its cities into an armed camp, rumbling through the streets in its Armored Personnel Carriers, shooting its machine guns and cannon at "anything that moves" — in the classical military terminology. Notice how quickly these minions of the State impose compulsory curfews on its peaceful citizens, how they block off — in violation of all human liberties — whole areas of a city and prevent anyone from going in or out, how they shut down all liquor stores and ban all sales of liquor. The philosophy of the State was never so well expressed as in an order that went over the Newark police radios when it was felt that violence by the State's armed forces was insufficient: "Use your shotguns and revolvers. Use your shotguns and revolvers. That's what you have them for." And a voice answered back: "It's about time." There is the voice of the State.

A second point to realize is the background to the rebellion. Three things triggered the rioting: First, the ever-present evil of police brutality, a brutality which is endemic in the Negro ghetto areas, although those of us who are upper-middle-class whites feel it only tangentially and in passing (except if we happen to be radicals or "subversives"). Police brutality as a rampant, permanent fact should not surprise us, for any group given a legal monopoly on violence will proceed to use the violence and that monopoly as best and as often as it can. The other two issues that had angered the Negroes of Newark were both State aggressions against the Negro citizens who constitute a majority of the town, but have no power in its government. One was failure to appoint a Negro as secretary to the Board of Education of a town in which the school enrollment is over three-quarters Negro. Another, and far more important, was the plan of the Newark government to liquidate thousands of Negro homes in the center of the Negro district of the city to make way for a campus of the State's College of Medicine and Dentistry.

It is no accident, finally, that the Negro insurrection began after a Negro cab driver was beaten up and arrested by the police; and began as a mob attack, escalating from tomatoes to Molotov cocktails, upon the offending police station.

CHAPTER 13

Abolish Slavery! Part VI

Some varieties of slavery permeate American life today and go completely unrecognized — even by the staunchest libertarians. Take, for example, one flagrant case which, as far as I know, has never been attacked by even the most consistent individualist: *compulsory jury duty.*

Jury work may or may not be a noble task, but the vitally important point about this work is that it is conducted under slave conditions; for, though the term of slavery may be short, compulsory jury duty is slavery, nonetheless. Men are routed off their jobs and herded, under pain of prison, to the courts, where they must sit or do actual jury service for several weeks, at pay approximating that of an Asian coolie. What is this if not slavery, if not involuntary servitude?

Defenders of the compulsory jury system claim that juries should constitute a cross-section of the community, and that this would not occur if jury service were voluntary. In the first place, juries are never cross-sections of the community; they are invariably hand-picked by "preferred" occupations and income levels. It is rare, for example, to see an unemployed laborer on a jury even though he is precisely the sort of person who might be willing to serve, even at today's miniscule levels of pay.

But the important point is not that juries are invariably hand-picked and discriminatory; the important point is that jury service is involuntary servitude. Precisely *because* jury work is so important to the lives and properties of the people, it is vital to have people on juries who come there willingly and voluntarily. And it is vital, too, to pay them enough so that they would be willing to perform this service.

If its defenders are right, and the jury system cannot survive on a voluntary basis, then so much the worse for the jury system. Any institution that cannot survive based on freedom of labor is clearly not worth surviving.

If we are to draft juries for slave wages, why not draft our judges as well? Or draft lawyers in general? Lawyers, however, are exempt from compulsory jury slavery, and hence our law-makers, who are largely lawyers, tend to look benignly on this draft system.

CHAPTER 14

Civil War in July, 1967
Part I

Tanks rumbling through the streets, buildings sprayed wholesale with machine gun fire, the rubble pervading the cities looking like Germany in 1945, compulsory curfews and blockades imposed — who would have thought during the Age of Apathy in the 1950s that, a decade later, America would be reduced to this? And who can now deny that the Negroes in America are a colonized and occupied people? The tanks, the National Guardsmen and state police, the federal troops, are merely the outward manifestation of this ever-present fact.

Ask yourself: If a white neighborhood were rioting and looting, would buildings be pulverized en masse by state and federal troops, wounding and killing thousands of innocent people? Would curfews be imposed and streets blockaded? Would apartment-to-apartment searches be made, as at Plainfield, New Jersey, breaking down doors and destroying furniture without bothering about search warrants? Of the thousands wounded during this virtual civil war of July, 1967, almost all were Negroes, and the vast majority were shot by trigger-happy white troops, concerned only to "shoot everything that is black and that moves," in the words of one officer. Since the greatest degree of devastation and shooting was performed by the state troops, we are justified in calling the July civil war an exercise in mass counter-revolutionary violence perpetrated by the government, in response to a far more limited Negro rebellion against a white state. For when the very basis of the state is challenged, or seems to be, the state's violence is many times that of the rebels.

And ask yourself also: By what right does the state move in and shoot looters? Surely looting cannot be condoned, but capital punishment for looting, which is what shooting amounts to, is just as criminal and unjustifiable. In my view, a criminal forfeits the rights which he takes away from another person; and therefore a murderer, who takes away from another person his right to life, deserves capital punishment. But surely, and by any known moral standards, capital punishment for mere robbery is so far excessive a punishment that it, in turn, amounts to criminal murder of the victim. We all revile the days of pre-Industrial Revolution Britain, when petty thieves were executed. Are we to return to that brutality now?

Perhaps the most incredible aspect of the July warfare was the decree of the mayor of Milwaukee — one that was universally applauded — forcing everyone off the streets! This, to be sure, ended the riot, but what did it do to the liberty of everyone in Milwaukee? Can we tolerate a country where no one is allowed on the streets because someone might commit a crime? The mayor only ended rioting in Milwaukee by turning that city into one vast jailhouse, and free men cannot tolerate this sort of action.

If the Negroes in America are, indeed, an occupied and colonized people, then we must give serious consideration to a solution which, baldly stated, seems absurd and ridiculous: the partitioning of the United States into white and Negro nations. This solution will be explored in future columns.

CHAPTER 15

Civil War in July, 1967 Part II

The most revealing fact of the July civil war in the American cities was the continuing parallel to the attitudes and actions of America's imperial war in Vietnam. The American troops' attitudes toward the Negroes in the urban ghettoes followed with uncanny similarity their attitudes toward that other oppressed colored people: the Vietnamese. This is apart from the fact that American Negroes are drafted to fight and die in disproportionate numbers in the Vietnam War.

Newsmen reported that, on New Jersey Governor [Richard J.] Hughes's staff during the fighting, there were the "hawks" and the "doves." Terms like "hold and clear," "search and destroy," began to be applied. Revealing also was the famous interview (*New York Times*, July 29) with Maj. Gen. Almerin C. O'Hara, commander of the New York State Army National Guard. General O'Hara called for a "greater commitment of force" to bring riots under control, and added the amazing statement that he would "not rule out the use of any weapon."

Escalation once more raises its ugly head; will someone soon suggest the use of tactical nuclear weapons on American cities? "Clean" ones, of course, so that the fallout doesn't filter down to white areas.

The General, however, assures us that while he contemplates the use of hand grenades, bazookas, and recoilless rifles, the chances of using heavy artillery are "very remote." Well, we must be grateful for small blessings.

General O'Hara insisted that National Guard actions must be under the authority and decisions of the military, including choice of tactics and weapons, since "civilians are not cognizant" of these delicate fine points. "These are military decisions which should be left to military men." O'Hara also stressed that the National Guard must not be "unduly restrained by civilian authority," because "if the military is brought in and they lose control, then what do you have left?"

The answer, it would appear, is no control at all, and in a supposedly "freedom-loving" country, is *that* so unthinkable?

General O'Hara conceded that the standard riot control techniques —stressing closed formations with bayonets at the ready — are "not really adequate for the kind of guerrilla warfare (these are American cities, remember, *not* Vietnam) and snipers we face these days." Instead he said that "military methods used in flushing guerrillas out of a village in Vietnam could be adapted to guerrilla warfare in the ghettoes."

"Of course," he added wistfully, "we can't do just what we would do in Vietnam. Out there if you had a sniper in a room you'd just crank up a tank and fire a shell through the window, destroying the whole room, and much of the building. I don't think public opinion would accept the use of that kind of force here."

Poor General O'Hara. To be hobbled like that! But cheer up, General. I'm afraid that public opinion might well support that kind of force — provided, of course, that it would not be used in white, middle-class areas. If *that* ever happened, you'd really have trouble on your hands.

CHAPTER 16

Civil War in July, 1967 Part III

Masterpiece of Unconscious Humor during the July Days: the unmitigated gall of President Johnson in his July 24 proclamation: "We will not endure violence. It matters not by whom it is done, or under what slogan or banner. It will not be tolerated."

Let us savor that statement, surely a classic of its kind. It is a statement from a man in charge of the greatest violence-wielding machine, the mightiest collection of destructive power, in the history of the world. It comes from a man in charge of the day-by-day use of that power to bomb, burn, and napalm thousands of innocent women and children and old people in Vietnam. For such a statement to come, in all seriousness, from the greatest violence-wielder of our time, and to be taken with a straight face by the public, demonstrates how far our society has gone down the road to irrationality. So, "it matters not by whom it is done, or under what slogan or banner," eh, Mr. President? Does that include the banner of "saving" the crushed and bleeding people of Vietnam from "International Communism"?

And so here we have our President making a totally absurd, irrational, and self-contradictory statement about violence, which no one seems to think is in the least out of order.

Let us contrast to this, the Masterpiece of Conscious Humor of the Month, and the clarity and sanity of this statement, by a supposedly irrational Negro extremist, H. Rap Brown, head of SNCC [Student Nonviolent Coordinating Committee]. Brown was asked at a press conference what it would take to satisfy black power militants. Brown replied: "I want Lyndon Johnson to resign and go to Vietnam and fight — he and his family." The reporter adds that "Negro onlookers cheered as he brushed aside newsmen's requests that he be 'more specific.'" Surely Brown cannot be blamed for this brushing aside; how specific can one get?

The Negro movement has come a long way from the days when compulsory integration was the goal and the NAACP was the leader. The old civil rights movement was thoroughly statist and modern-liberal; its goal was to use the arm of the federal and other governments to coerce whites into hiring, eating, and living with Negroes. The new movement, headed by Rap Brown and Stokely Carmichael of SNCC, is totally and radically alienated from the government of the United States and the entire "power structure." To contrast, once more, two statements of LBJ and H. Rap Brown, LBJ proclaimed: "From its earliest day, our nation has been dedicated to justice, to equality — and to order," while Brown declared: "The white man makes all the laws, he drags us before his courts, he accuses us, and he sits in judgment over us."

There speaks the voice of a true black nationalist; and the logic of black nationalism, finally explicitly stated in the National Black Power Conference at Newark this July, is a national black republic totally separated and seceded from the US government. As absurd as this goals seems when first stated, this is the inner logic of the continuing rebellions of the Negro ghettoes, and this is the direction in which these rebellions are, willy-nilly, moving. For the other traditional solutions are not going to work. The conservative solution of ever-greater force it not going to work, for during the rioting it was the entry of the National Guard that stimulated and accelerated the retaliatory sniping; the conservative solution cannot work, short of exterminating the entire Negro population.

And nothing is deader than the liberal solution of more federal funds, more playgrounds, and the rest of the liberal pap. Detroit was supposed to be the great model home of Liberal Race Relations, with plenty of playgrounds, inter-racial committees, and all the rest. And Detroit suffered a week-long civil war and property damage of $1 billion. Detroit murdered liberalism, and good riddance.

CHAPTER 17

The Principle of Secession

General de Gaulle has been reviled, derided, and hooted at by the entire American press for getting up in Quebec and shouting, "*Vive le Quebec Libre*" (Long Live a Free Quebec!). For the American mind seems totally incapable of understanding the principle of secession or the desire of an oppressed ethnic minority to separate and liberate itself from the tyranny of the majority. In the United States everybody laughed and called de Gaulle a senile, doddering old fool; but in Canada, and above all in Quebec, nobody laughed. They were either angry and bitter, or they cheered; but they didn't laugh. For they knew that Canada is two nations, and that the British have been dominating the French in Canada ever since Britain invaded and conquered New France (as Canada was called) in the mid-eighteenth century.

Why *shouldn't* the French of Quebec have the right to secede from Canada and form their own nation, where their own language and culture prevails? None of the territorial boundaries of the current governments of the world are God-ordained; they are all products of historical forces, most of which were unjust and coercive, with many resulting in oppressed minorities and plundering majorities. There is every reason, then, why these boundaries and state areas should be changed to conform more with the principles of freedom and justice.

Many libertarians cannot understand why one should take any stand on such a matter as secession. Wouldn't the French only be setting up a Quebec state, and why would this better than a Canadian state? One answer is that decentralization is itself a good, because the Canadian state will then be weakened and deprived of power over a territorial area; the more states the world is fragmented into, the less power any one state can build up, either over its own hapless subjects or over foreign peoples in making war.

But another answer is that as long as states exist it is a net gain to eliminate the tyranny of a state over a minority ethnic group, and the secession of that group into its own state is therefore an important net gain for freedom. And there is another important reason for hailing the principle of secession *per se*: for if one part of a country is allowed to secede, and this principle is established, then a sub-part of that must be allowed to secede, and a sub-part of *that*, breaking the government into ever smaller and less powerful fragments ... until at last the principle is established that *the individual* may secede — and then we will have true freedom at last.

And on so many grounds: principle, ethnic freedom, pragmatic destruction of State Leviathan power, ultimate principle of individual secession, it is incumbent upon every lover of liberty to hail secession movements wherever and however they may arise. Therefore, let us hail them all: the Quebec Liberation Movement, Scottish nationalism, Welsh nationalism, the secession of the Ibo people of Eastern Nigeria into the independent republic of Biafra, the "left-wing" secession of the Eastern Congo and the "right-wing" secession of Katanga and, last but not least, the prospect of a black republic seceding from the U.S. Hence the tragedy of the southern defeat in the Civil War, for that defeat has buried the very thought of secession in this country from that time forward. But might does not make right, and the cause of secession may rise again.

CHAPTER 18

Should There Be a Tax Hike? Part I

Conservatives and libertarians alike suffer from a failure to recognize who is responsible for the accelerating march of this country into statism. Ayn Rand once wrote that big business is "America's most persecuted minority." Nothing could be further from the truth.

From the turn of the twentieth century, through the New Deal period, and up to the present day, big business has been in the forefront of the shift from a free economy and a free society toward statism. For it saw in the state what the mercantilists —the big businessmen of *their* day — saw: a golden opportunity to confer upon themselves special privileges through subsidies, monopolies, cartels, contracts, etc. Two brilliant books of recent years — both by historian Gabriel Kolko, *Triumph of Conservatism* and *Railroads and Regulation* — have shown conclusively that the government regulations of the Progressive period around 1900, from which grew the Great Society of today, were *not* brought about to curb big business "monopoly." Instead, various powerful big businessmen, disappointed in their attempts to gain monopoly on the free market, turned to the federal government to impose such monopolies and cartels in the guise of "progressive" reforms.

Out of these regulations and controls has emerged the veritable corporate state of today — a society and economy run by Big Government in partnership with Big Business and Big Unions — with the average citizen getting it in the neck. It is a corporate state with a "welfare" and "progressive" rhetoric, which some of the New Left historians have perceptively called a system of "corporate liberalism;" in short the reality of a corporate state cloaked in "liberal" and "welfare" ideology.

There is nothing that the American economy or the American people need *less* than another income tax hike. Yet now that President Johnson has suggested a ten percent tax increase, the legions of Big Business have come leaping to its defense.

The National Association of Manufacturers, once a sturdy opponent of statism and Big Government, has endorsed an income tax rise; perhaps it is not a coincidence that the president of the NAM, W. P. Gullander, who has been trumpeting the "positive" program of "partnership" between Big Business and Big Government, comes to the NAM from a term as head of General Dynamics, a corporation virtually built out of government funds and government contracts. A less free-market-oriented corporation would be difficult to imagine.

And now we find that 113 of the biggest big businessmen in the country — including David Rockefeller, Henry Ford II, and the heads of AT&T, General Electric, and General Motors — are organizing a group to press for full support of Johnson's ten percent income tax increase.

They are certainly not *acting* like "America's most persecuted minority." On the contrary, we must give these men credit for knowing on which side their bread is buttered.

CHAPTER 19

Should There Be a Tax Hike? Part II

The big argument for an income tax increase now is one taken from Lord Keynes: during a boom the government should raise income taxes in order to "sop up excess purchasing power" and prevent inflation. There are many fallacies in this argument for a tax hike.

The first problem is in identifying the current economic scene as a boom. The point is, if we look at such key indicators as corporate profits and investments, we are *still* in a recession. Everybody expects an upturn soon, but the upturn hasn't occurred yet. And even if it does, the boom will still be so weak that a ten percent income tax increase may well be just enough to break the boom and precipitate a really severe recession because tax increases lower the incentive to save, invest, and produce.

But apart from this problem of timing and forecasting, there are more serious errors in the Keynesian call for a tax increase in a boom. The main problem is that price rises are brought about by inflation of the supply of money — and in our virtually nationalized banking system totally under the federal government's control, this means that the government has pumped more money into the economy. The effect is something like diluting a powerful chemical mixture: if you pump more dollars into the economy, then each dollar will be worth less in purchasing power. In short, prices will go up. The trick is this: *first* the government creates new money, spends it or has it loaned out to its favorite groups; *then*, when the new money inevitably results in higher prices, the government turns around and denounces all sorts of social groups for *spending* this new money. The blame for the "excess purchasing power" is thus cunningly taken from the shoulders of the real culprit — government — and placed onto the shoulders of various groups in the economy. In fact, different groups are encouraged to quarrel among themselves with, for example, labor unions blaming businessmen for the higher prices and businessmen attempting to blame the demands of trade unions. All this time the real culprit — government — takes on the mantle of the savior of society from all these greedy price-increasing groups. In its role of savior, government then comes up with the notion of a tax increase to "sop up" the purchasing power.

Look at what government is doing: *first* it burdens the citizens by inflating the money supply and thereby raising prices; *then* it imposes a double burden by turning around and taxing away much of the new money. The people are skewered twice.

The theory of the tax increase implies, furthermore, that taxes are no burden at all, certainly no burden in comparison with a higher price. If the price of a good or service goes up, however, while this may be unfortunate, *at least* we're still getting the useful good or service for our money. But if a *tax* goes up, to save us from the bad old price increase, what have we gotten in return for this burden? Nothing, since no one can pretend that the "benefit" we get from government increases proportionately to the tax. In fact we get a negative return from government, since the government will only use the new income to regulate, harass, and otherwise push us around.

Finally, not only is a higher tax worse than a higher price, but a government deficit, contrary to the Keynesians, is not necessarily inflationary. It is only inflationary if the deficit is financed by the banking system; if it is financed by selling bonds to the public, it will have other unfortunate effects, but it won't increase the money supply or raise prices. So don't let Keynesian sophists fool you. Higher taxes means higher robbery, and that benefits neither the public nor the state of the economy.

CHAPTER 20

Abolish Slavery! Part VII

On any definition, "slavery" means forced labor.

One of the most pervasive cases of forced labor in America today is the withholding tax. Under the withholding tax, the employer is coerced by the government into recording and collecting his employees' income tax, and turning that tax over to the authorities. Not only is this labor coerced by the government, but also that labor is totally unpaid. It is slave labor with no return. The withholding tax is a crucial element in that mass instrument of robbery known as the income tax. For before World War II, when the income tax was much lower and far fewer people were forced to pay it, there was no withholding tax at all. Every man counted up his tax at the end of the year and then was supposed to pay the government in a lump sum. As the income tax rose astronomically during the war, the federal government shrewdly imposed the withholding tax, forcing the employer to collect the tax as deductions from his workers' salaries.

It is quite clear that if withholding-tax-slavery were abolished, the entire mammoth income tax robbery would fall to the ground. For the reason that the government can collect the tax smoothly is that each man does not have to get up the money in a lump sum; rather it is smoothly and seemingly painlessly extracted from him as he earns, so that he hardly realizes what is happening. If every man had to pay in a lump sum on April

15, mass evasion and non-payment would be so widespread that the entire system would break down.

It is instructive to remember a long-forgotten fact: that the withholding tax, suggested by Beardsley Ruml of R.H. Macy and Company, was supposed to be a wartime emergency measure only. It was accepted as a wartime emergency measure; and now, a generation later, it is not only still with us, but is a permanent and unchallenged part of our way of life.

The slavery of record-keeping and tax-paying holds also throughout the rest of the economy. Every businessman is forced to spend a great deal of time and money filling out endless forms and records for countless branches of government; federal, state, and local. He is forced to expend his labor without pay. These costs levied on everyone especially injure and hamper *small* business, which can far less afford the time and energy than can a large corporation.

Furthermore, every man, when he is forced to fill out his income tax return every year, must expend many hours of unpaid labor to figure out his own degree of victimization. And not only the income tax: the sales and other excise taxes are collected and paid by the retailers, and so they too must expend many hours of unpaid labor to collect taxes for the government.

Forced labor can never be expunged from our society until this compulsory tax-paying and collecting, this coerced record-keeping, is swept away.

CHAPTER 21

Businessmen For Peace

One of the most heartening developments on the current American scene is the new nation-wide organization, Business Executives Move for a Vietnam Peace. These dedicated businessmen came from all over the country to meet at the Statler-Hilton in Washington on September 27, to form their organization and expressed their determined and cogent opposition to the war in Vietnam. There were none of the very big businessmen represented here — none of the Rockefellers, Watsons, or Weinbergs — in short, none of the big businessmen tied in with the federal government and its machine for war spending and war contracts. These were the middle-rank executives throughout the country, presidents of their own firms, genuinely tied in with the free, private market economy.

It is one of the widespread socialist canards that wars are brought about by the capitalist economy; that wars are inherent in the private enterprise system. The truth is really the reverse: since the rise of business enterprise, this system has been one of the requisites and mainstays of free trade, free markets, and international peace. All of these go hand in hand. But, as one cynic once shrewdly said, "The only thing wrong with capitalism is the capitalists," and particular capitalists have often turned to the state to promote wars for their own benefit. In doing so, they have given the capitalist system as a whole an undeservedly bad name. Now these businessmen have come forward to redeem that name.

The most publicized speech at this gathering was made by Senator Thruston Morton (R., Ky.), who has so far embraced the cause of peace, in contrast to his usual bland and mild position on public affairs, that he accused President Johnson of being "brainwashed" to extend the war, and he particularly pinpointed the sinister influence of that "military-industrial complex" that President Eisenhower warned us of in his clearest and most penetrating public address. Morton's speech reflects a growing and pervasive shift toward peace by congressional Republicans, sparked by the much-abused Republication staff White Paper on Vietnam a few months ago. Doubtless these Republicans remember that Eisenhower was elected in 1952 largely on his "I will go to Korea" pledge, which led to the ending of the Korean holocaust.

Even harder-hitting was the address to the businessmen's group by Marriner S. Eccles, San Francisco and Utah businessman and former head of the Federal Reserve Board. Eccles stressed that the Vietnam war was causing a huge federal deficit, an increase in income taxes, and higher costs of living. On the Vietcong, Eccles declared: "They are fighting for national liberation and unity of South Vietnam: the causes for which others, including Americans; have fought." He added:

> To withdraw is sanity. [Applause] The consequences of withdrawing cannot possibly be as disastrous for this nation as pursuing our present course. [Applause] The greatest service we could render the Vietnamese is to withdraw from their country, leaving them to negotiate a conclusion to the war, which is their right. [Applause]

And Admiral Arnold True (Ret.) warned the businessmen that unless American foreign policy was completely changed and stopped supporting dictatorships everywhere, we'd be faced with many "Vietnams" in Africa, Asia, and Latin America.

Business Executives Move for Vietnam Peace can be contacted through Harold Willens, President, Factory Equipment Supply Co., Los Angeles; or Henry E. Niles, Chairman, Baltimore Life Insurance Co.

CHAPTER 22

"Incitement" To Riot

H. Rap Brown, fiery young leader of SNCC, has been indicted in Cambridge, Maryland for the "crime" of "incitement to riot" There are few of us who have sat down to analyze what exactly this "crime" is supposed to be. Suppose that Mr. A tells Mr. B: "Go out and shoot the mayor." Suppose, then, that Mr. B, pondering this suggestion, decides it's a darn good idea and goes out and shoots the mayor. Now obviously B is responsible for the shooting. But in what sense can A be held responsible? A did not do the shooting, and didn't take part, we will assume, in any of the planning or executing of the act itself. The very fact that he made that suggestion cannot really mean that A should be held responsible. For does not B have free will? Is he not a free agent? And if he is, then B and B alone is responsible for the shooting.

If we attribute any responsibility at all to A, we have fallen into the trap of determinism. We are then assuming that B has no will of his own, that he is then only a tool in some way manipulated by A. Now I dare say that most of the people who are anxious to prosecute Rap Brown for "incitement to riot" are religious people. But if they are religious, they must believe in the individual's freedom of will, a fundamental concept of Jewish and Christian religions. But if the will is free, then no man is determined by another; then just because somebody shouts "burn, baby, burn," no one hearing this advice is thereby compelled or determined to go and carry the suggestion out. Anybody who does carry out the advice is responsible for his own actions, and *solely* responsible. Therefore, the "inciter" cannot be held in any way responsible. In the nature of man and morality, there is no such crime as "incitement to riot," and therefore the very concept of such a "crime" should be stricken from the statute books.

Cracking down on "incitement to riot," then, is simply and purely cracking down on one's natural and crucial right to freedom of speech. Speech is not a crime. And hence the injustice, not only of the crime of incitement, but also of such other "crimes" as "criminal sedition" (sharp criticism of the government), or "conspiracy to advocate overthrow of the government" — in other words, planning someday to exercise one's basic and natural right to freedom of speech and advocacy.

CHAPTER 23

Gun Laws

Every time someone is conspicuously shot in America, every time some maniac starts splattering people with a rifle or machine gun, various propagandists move in to whip up hysteria and call for severe government restrictions on the purchase or possession of guns. Never mind that such laws and ordinances are clearly unconstitutional, for the Constitution clearly and flatly guarantees the right of the people to bear arms. This right has always been considered crucial to the liberties of the people from government oppression; for if all the guns are surrendered to one organized group — the government — the freedoms of all are in jeopardy from those who have acquired a monopoly of the weapons of violence. For, as in the classical query, "Who is to guard our guardians?" The Sullivan and other laws were the first chink in the dike; the excuse for these patently unconstitutional and despotic laws was that there was something uniquely sinister about "concealed" weapons that deserves restriction. Now this is to be extended to unconcealed weaponry.

The theory is that if private guns are restricted or outlawed, crimes of violence using guns would be eliminated. What a silly doctrine! One would think that we had learned the lesson of Prohibition: outlawry of liquor did not end the use of liquor, nor has outlawry of narcotics ended their widespread use. The upshot of these restrictions and prohibitions is that the honest person, the innocent citizen, the non-alcoholic or nonaddict, is prevented from buying or using guns or alcohol. The addict, the alcoholic, or the criminal are not deterred by the law. They have their sources, and they are always able to get their supply. No criminal, no Mafia member, has been stopped from getting revolvers because of the Sullivan or other such laws. The result is that while criminals continue to be plentifully supplied with guns, the non-criminal, the man who wants to buy a gun to defend himself from crime, is prevented from doing so: so the law renders him helpless in the face of crime.

Such is typically the result of "do-gooding" legislation, where actions or purchases are outlawed for somebody's "own good." The result is that, for his "own good," he's left at the criminal's mercy.

The revolver used to be called "the equalizer," and so it is. Without such a weapon the weak, the frail, the elderly, and women, can not compete with the muscles and clubs of strong-arm criminals, even if the latter do not have guns. But women and the frail and the aged *can* shoot straight, and this gives them much more of a chance in the jungles that many of our cities have become. If he knows that his victim may be armed, the mugger or the rapist will think twice before attacking; now it is open season.

There is, finally, no sense in outlawing a particular weapon such as a gun. There are lots of things which can be used and have been used as weapons. Where are we to stop? Shall we outlaw knives, sticks, bricks, or what? When will we realize that crime lies, not in the *object*, but in the way in which that or any object may be used?

CHAPTER 24

LBJ — After Four Years

Well, this month marks our fourth full year of the presidential rule of Lyndon Baines Johnson, and it is high time to sum up his reign. These four years have been years of enormous frustration and resentment on the part of America's liberal intellectual community. Here was a man who looked and still looks upon FDR as his political mentor — a man who ran with the support of the ADA [Americans for Democratic Action], of old and new New Dealers, of all authentic liberals — and here is a man who is now universally reviled by those former supporters.

The whole saga is very reminiscent of the way Trotsky and his followers felt betrayed by Stalin. The horror and brutality of the Stalin era were felt to be some sort of monstrous perversion, some inexplicable intrusion into the original Lenin-Trotsky ideal. And now the horrors and warmongering of Johnson are felt to be another inexplicable betrayal of Roosevelt-Truman-Kennedy liberalism.

But the situation is not that simple, as uncomfortable as this truth will be for our liberal friends. Stalin was the logical outgrowth of the "ideals" of Lenin and Trotsky. In the same way, Lyndon Baines Johnson was and still is a liberal through and through. By launching imperial war against foreign countries, by expanding the power of the state over the economy and the society, by bringing ever greater military control of society, Lyndon

Baines Johnson is only following in the footsteps of his — and the intellectuals' — beloved mentors, Roosevelt and Truman. No wonder Lyndon feels puzzled and betrayed by the rancor of the liberal intellectuals! He is only doing what they and their mentors taught him: he is expanding unchecked presidential power in foreign and domestic affairs and launching imperial global crusades in the name of "world freedom" and "collective security." So why the fuss and feathers?

The liberals have got to wake up to the great truth that Lyndon Baines Johnson is liberalism in action-liberalism personified. This instructive lesson will be lost upon them if they grow increasingly horrified at his despotic and dangerous rule; if they do not realize that what they are seeing is not a personal aberration of the Devil, but the ultimate triumph of their own liberal principles. If they don't like what they see, they must abandon liberalism, and rapidly.

Meanwhile, the conservatives could use a lot of soul-searching, too. Whatever they had in anti-statist principles has long been swept away, sacrificed on the altar of the latter-day crusade against the Communist wing of statism. Conservative enthusiasm for Johnson and his cohorts can be gauged by the enormous conservative support for Senator Thomas Dodd (D., Conn.), a man with a virtually 100 percent ADA-liberal record. The old categories are dissolving fast.

CHAPTER 25

A New Constitution?

In recent years the nation's conservatives, bitter and angry at Supreme Court decisions preserving the rights of the individual against the police, have begun to demand a new Constitutional convention which could totally rewrite our present document. Rubbing their hands with glee, the conservatives have believed that the new convention would devote itself to such cherished conservative tasks as: (1) making sure that a rural voter gets several times the voting power of an urban or suburban voter, and (b) allowing the police to run roughshod over the rights of the citizen in the name of fighting crime. Why *libertarians* should devote themselves to either of these goals is, of course, a grim mystery.

The conservative view of the world is a curious one, and never has this fact been more glaring than in their drive for a new convention. Apparently, the conservatives either do not know or do not care that any new convention would obviously make our present charter much worse than it is — providing far more channels for state dictation over the individual. Or perhaps conservatives don't care how statist we become, so long as the police share a good chunk of the new governmental power.

At any rate, a good test of what would happen in any new convention occurred recently in New York State, which just concluded a Constitutional Convention of its own. The major achievements of "ConCon" are twofold: (1) removal of the public referendum barrier to new state and local bond issues, and (2) removal of the old Constitutional barrier against state aid to parochial schools.

[The first change] means that no longer will the people have the right and power to vote down the endless stream of school bond and other bond proposals which the big spenders in government spend their lives concocting. In recent years the people's power to vote on these boondoggles has proved a serious embarrassment to the Establishment, as bond after bond issue has been voted down — calling down the wrath of educationists, school boardsmen, intellectuals, and bankers who underwrite the bonds. Now the ConCon proposes to rid the State of New York of this annoying democratic encumbrance on its collective will.

The second major change proposes to put a serious breach in the important American principle of separation of church and state. This separation means that the state shall have no power to meddle in the religious life of the country — a perfectly exemplary principle that the libertarian would like to extend to other spheres of society as well. But the conservatives, of course, are in the forefront of wishing to bring the state and church together. In the process, the long-suffering taxpayer would be hit again, this time for subsidies to religious schools *not* of his choice.

It is instructive to see how left and right have divided in New York over this new Constitution. The civil-libertarian-left opposes it because of the parochial school plank; the budget-conscious-right opposes it because of the end of the referendum barrier to state spending. In the center are a mass of supporters — especially among Catholics — who approve heartily of both changes. The libertarian, of course, heartily *opposes* both, and therefore is more devoted than anyone to defeating the new Constitution. It will be interesting to see how this incipient left-right alliance against the statist Constitution fares in battle against the Establishmentarian center.

CHAPTER 26

The Elections

The 1967 elections present many heartening features. The main trend shining through is the confirmation of all recent public opinion polls: the disastrous plummeting of support for the Johnson administration. Never in recent history has a president been so mistrusted, deplored, and reviled by all segments of the population; his popularity has reached an all-time low in the polls.

Confirmation of this trend by the elections is clear: In New Jersey, for example, where Governor Richard Hughes has been closely identified with the Johnson Administration, a 2-1 Democratic majority in the legislature has been turned around to a phenomenal 3-1 Republican margin. In Kentucky, Louie Nunn has become the first Republic governor in decades, giving the Republican party a majority of the nation's governors. Nunn's main campaign thrust was opposition to the administration's war in Vietnam, and it is clear that the Vietnam war has played a large, if not dominant, role in the growing repudiation of the President. Contrary to most of the interpretation in the press, the 33 percent vote in the San Francisco referendum for immediate withdrawal from Vietnam is a victory for the anti-war forces: for this is a position too advanced for a large part of the Vietnam critics, much less the general population.

On the other great issue of our epoch — the race question — the elections, again contrary to the press, were a repudiation of the administration.

For while it is true that the Negroes Carl Stokes and Richard Hatcher won the mayoralty races in Cleveland and in Gary, Indiana, with the blessings of the administration, the important point is that they squeaked through in overwhelmingly Democratic cities. All this points up the Democratic collapse and the continuing Republican resurgence.

And in New York the voters of the state delivered a smashing 3 to 1 repudiation of the proposed state Constitution. The vote was an unofficial alliance of left and right against the center, headed by the Democratic Party of New York State; the Constitution would have prevented voters from passing on state bond issues, and would have given state aid to private and parochial schools.

Finally, to complete the picture of Democratic disarray and disintegration, the conscientious Senator Eugene McCarthy (D., Minn.) is reportedly getting ready to challenge President Johnson in the 1968 primaries — a remarkable step, growing out of the increasing despair of thoughtful Democrats at the escalating road to ruin in Vietnam.

In the midst of this picture, all the Republicans need do is to present a reasonable choice in 1968 to gain victory. But the curious situation is that there is no leading Republican candidate for the presidency who reflects in any way the growing public disgust with the war in Vietnam, or even the growing peace sentiment (led by the powerful Senator Thruston Morton, R., Ky.) within the party itself.

Clearly the Republican way to victory next year is the same as Eisenhower's "I Will Go to Korea" pledge in 1952; with that pledge, Ike established himself as the peace candidate, a peace that he indeed brought about as soon as he took office.

But every leading candidate for 1968 either endorses the Johnson war or wants to escalate it still further — all except Governor [George W.] Romney, who seems invincibly confused on the whole question. The only peaceish candidates are Senators [Mark] Hatfield (R., Ore.) and [Charles] Percy (R., Ill.) and General [James M.] Gavin, all the darkest of dark horses.

And so the Republican Party might well continue to nourish its almost uninterrupted genius for self-destruction.

CHAPTER 27

Why Do They All Hate De Gaulle?

When the Establishment Press really zeroes in on someone and smites him from pillar to post, day after day, then it is a safe bet that he can't be all bad. It is also a wise move to dig further and find out the reason for all this uniform wrath. So in the case of Charles de Gaulle, whom the press, liberal and conservative, has been denouncing and vilifying for years.

Why? Well for one thing, conservatives feel that they have been betrayed. The right wing is perpetually on the hunt for a Strong Man, a Man on a White Horse, who will come and, by stern dictatorial measure, bring us forth to our true rightist mission of National Glory and World Crusade. The right was therefore delighted when a coup brought down the Fourth Republic in France and elevated General de Gaulle to a quasi-dictatorial post over the French nation. Here was a man with seemingly all the qualifications to be beloved of the right wing: a general; a grandiloquent national patriot filled with the rhetoric and the mystique of French national grandeur; a man who tied in his own personal sense of glory with France itself. Who better?

It was at that point when the right received its shock. For "*le grand Charlie*," instead of instituting rightist measures, proceeded on a very intelligent and sensible course. De Gaulle had learned the lesson of the crippling defeat of the French empire in Indo-China. He had learned that, in spite of his own personal preference for Glory and Empire, France in this day and age could not afford the cost, financial and political, of trying to hold onto rule in places where the native population had risen up to win its independence. And so de Gaulle decided to adjust to the new world, to pull completely out of the French empire in Algeria, and to make genuine peace with the lands formerly in colonial subjection. The wrath of the right, both in France and the U.S., at de Gaulle has never abated since.

He dared to pull out where France was not wanted and to grant the natives their independence! And ever since, as at Quebec, de Gaulle has become a firm partisan of the struggles for independence by all of the Third World, including his courageous support of the Arab cause in the Middle East.

In Europe, too, de Gaulle decided that it was far better for all to abandon the American-induced posture of hostility and division between the East and West power blocs. Clearly, it would be better for all of Europe, East and West, to live in peace and harmony, and to opt out of the damaging and potentially catastrophic cold war struggle. Hence, de Gaulle's persisting attempts to achieve friendship and peaceful co-existence with Soviet Russia and Eastern Europe.

In contrast, de Gaulle, angry at American imperialism's attempts to push France and every other western nation around, declared for genuine political independence from the U.S. Hence the anger of the Liberal Establishment toward France.

And last but not least, de Gaulle's admirable political independence has been matched by a healthy economic independence, best expressed by his firm refusal, in the face of maximum political pressure by the United State, to go along with Anglo-American policies of easy money and inflation. Guided by the libertarian economist and monetary expert Jacques Rueff, de Gaulle has fought the good fight, almost alone, for hard money and for a return to a genuine gold standard at a realistically valued rate (e.g., $70 or so per ounce instead of the current absurd rate of $35).

De Gaulle has, virtually single-handedly, stood between all of us and an eventually disastrous worldwide inflation propelled by Britain and the United States. These are some of the reasons by the Establishment, both right and left, hates de Gaulle, and why the rest of us should not.

CHAPTER 28

The Cyprus Question

Turk and Greek are once again threatening war over Cyprus. No patchwork peace settlement will last. In the United States, both the left and the right are confused; since there is manifestly no Communist issue involved, and since Communism dominates everyone's thinking, neither rightists nor leftists are able to come to grips with the complex of rights and wrongs involved.

The problem begins, as do so many other problems in the world, with British imperialism. Britain occupied and ruled Cyprus until 1960, and the ethnic problem on the island festered until that date. While the Greeks outnumber the Turks by four to one on the island as a whole, there is a clear and evident solution to the conflict in personalities, ethnic ties, language, and culture that sunders the two ethnic groups. That solution is partition, because Cyprus is dotted with a number of self-contained Greek and Turkish towns and communities, with virtually no integration within each town; in the capital city of Nicosia, the northern quarter is exclusively Turk and the rest of the town is Greek.

When Britain was preparing to grant the island independence, the Turks, instead of urging partition, alienated the Greek patriots by pressing Britain to maintain its rule rather than leave the Turkish minority to Greek mercies. But the independence agreement, while failing to grant partition, did have the merit of granting the Turkish communities autonomy in their areas, and giving Turks veto power over Cypriote legislation. But the Greek Cypriotes were not content with this fairly equitable arrangement. The Cypriote regime began to infringe on the agreed autonomy; worse, the government, in collaboration with mainland Greece, systematically and grievously violated the agreed limitation on the number of mainland troops on the island. While Britain, the Greeks, and the Turks had agreed to limit mainland armed forces on the island to 950 (with Turkey allowed a lower quota), the Greeks, under the command of the fervent and fascistic General [Giorgios] Grivas, infiltrated from six to twelve thousand troops onto the island. This infiltration raised for the Turks the dread spectre of *enosis* — of union of Cyprus with the Greek mainland, which would completely jeopardize Turkish autonomy.

Through a series of crises, this troop concentration has been built up. Further, since 1962 the Turkish communities, again in violation of their autonomy, have been blockaded by the Greek troops. In the guise of keeping the Turkish minority from acquiring "strategic materials," the Greek soldiers have prevented them from possessing timber, spare auto parts, cement, telephones, jackets, shoes, and raincoats. Finally, as the last straw, General Grivas recently retaliated against some Turkish snipers by massacring whole Turkish villages. That massacre touched off the current Cypriote crisis.

It is clear from our history of the problem that the Turks have legitimate grievances of long standing, and that the problem won't be set aright until partition insures the absolute protection of the rights of the Turkish people. In this crisis the United States, true to its long-standing policy of defending the status quo whatever it may be, has for years come down squarely on the side of the Greek rulers over the Turkish minorities. Hence, the burning of the American flag by angry students in the Turkish capital of Ankara. America, once again, almost unerringly, comes down on the wrong side — and again, unsurprisingly, its U.N. vote on behalf of freezing the status quo lined it up side by side with the Soviet Union.

CHAPTER 29

How To Get Out of Vietnam

A lot of people throughout the country are beginning to realize that getting into the Vietnam war was a disastrous mistake. In fact, hardly anyone makes so bold as to justify America's entrance into, and generation of, that perpetual war. And so the last line of defense for the war's proponents is: Well, maybe it was a mistake to get into the war, but now that we're there, we're committed, so we have to carry on.

A curious argument. Usually, in life, if we find out that a course of action has been a mistake, we abandon that course and try something else. This is supposed to be the time-honored principle of "trial and error." Or if a business project or investment turns out to be an unprofitable venture, we abandon it and try investing elsewhere. Only in the Vietnam war do we suddenly find that, having launched a disaster, we are stuck with it forevermore and must continue to pour in blood and treasure until eternity.

But just *who* are we committed to, anyway? Surely not the South Vietnamese government, for whatever puppet was induced to "invite" us in has gone long ago, deposed or assassinated. Surely not the people of South Vietnam, the overwhelming majority of whom either back the National Liberation Front or who, at the very least, give no support whatever to our favorite dictator, Marshall [Nguyen Cao] Ky. If we are out to liberate or defend these people, then we are doing it in a most curious way: namely, by a continuing and apparently permanent process of subjecting them to our methods of mass murder and destruction. "Liberation" — through mass killing and devastation!

We are left with the woeful tale of a few hundred thousand Vietnamese who are committed to the U.S. side; what will become of them when the NLF takes over? Well, there is a happy way out for these people: the U.S. can offer to transport them here, where they can enjoy the benefits of the American Way of Life first-hand. Of course, if this suggestion were ever made, then all of our war-hawks who bleed so profusely for the South Vietnamese at Communism's door would suddenly find all sorts of reasons for not letting these same free-world citizens into the sacred portals of the U.S.A. It wasn't long ago, of course, that Orientals were barred completely from immigrating to the United States, and this coercive, racist exclusion was upheld by many of the very same people who want all of us to die in defense of these same Orientals, against the "world conspiracy."

But how can we get out of Vietnam? Johnson, too, claims to be for peace, but he complains that in all the morass of negotiations or would-be negotiations, he can't find a way. Well, the way is mere child's play: the way to get out of Vietnam is to get out. Period. Leave. Withdraw. Scram. And if the American people were to make this demand crystal clear, I'm sure that Johnson and the Pentagon would quickly find the knowledge of how to get our troops onto troopships and bring them home. The war crowd has been trumpeting the slogan, "Support Our Boys in Vietnam." Well, it seems clear to me that if we are really concerned with the welfare of our boys in Vietnam, the best we can do for them — as well as for the Vietnamese — is to get them out of that death trap and ship them home, and into civilian life.

Then everyone would be happy: Americans and Vietnamese — all except the fanatics who'd be happy to destroy the world rather than allow some Communist, somewhere, to stay alive. And maybe then we'd get used to a world, which existed not so long ago, where America would not decide the fate of every people and territory on the face of the globe.

CHAPTER 30

The Case of John Milton Ratliff

Ever since I was a little tot, General Lewis B. Hershey has been in charge of that selective slavery system known as the draft. The man seems ageless and, as in the case of that other seemingly Indispensable Man, J. Edgar Hoover, General Hershey's retirement rights were waived for the greater good of us all, and he rolls on, presumably immortal, ever calling out his creed of Draft 'Em All. The latest effusion of our Simon Legree was to urge the local draft boards to draft those youngsters who interfere with the workings of the Selective Service System. There is good ground to think that this edict is unconstitutional, since we are all supposed to be equal before the law, and the draft system is not supposed to be able to single out anyone it does not like for punishment.

But, in its wisdom, the Selective Service System has gone beyond the simple draft of those who illegally interfere with the draft process; it has now proceeded onward to drafting someone because, and *only* because, he is a member of an anti-war, anti-draft organization. If this act is allowed to stand, freedom of speech or of opposition to government policies in this country will be but a mockery.

Here is the story: On November 13, 1967, Local Board No. 76 of Tulsa, Oklahoma sent a letter to Mr. John Milton Ratliff of Norman, Oklahoma. It told Mr. Ratliff, a freshman at the University of Oklahoma, that it was rescinding his 2-S (student deferment) classification and classifying him

1-A, because the Selective Service regulations provide a 2-S for anyone whose "study is found to be necessary to the maintenance of the national health, safety or interest." The local board then added that is "did not feel that your activity as a member of SDS (Students for a Democratic Society, an anti-war, anti-draft organization) is to the best interest of the U.S. government."

So now it is not just illegal activity, but any determined opposition to U.S. policies that makes one subject to conscription. How can free speech be said to exist when this sort of oppression goes on?

Lt. Col. Charles Humphrey, manpower specialist at the Oklahoma Selective Service headquarters, conceded to reporters that Ratliff's reclassification was due to his anti-war activities. "You're aware of General Hershey's statement," he told a reporter. "He said because of their activities maybe they shouldn't be deferred and maybe we should look at it. So that's what the boards are doing."

So maybe *we* should take a look at the conscription system!

CHAPTER 31

Jim Garrison, Libertarian

In the welter of discussion (mainly abuse) on Jim Garrison's conspiracy case in the Kennedy assassination, an important story has been overlooked: the inspiring and knowledgeable devotion to individual liberty that has shone through Garrison's statements.

Thus, in the famous and impressive *Playboy* interview of October, 1967, Garrison said this about the role of District Attorney: "You know, I always received much more satisfaction as a defense attorney in obtaining an acquittal for a client than I ever have as a D.A. in obtaining a conviction. All my interests and sympathies tend to be on the side of the individual as opposed to the state."

On the political trends in contemporary America:

> What worries me deeply, and I have seen it exemplified in this case, is that we in America are in great danger of slowly evolving into a proto-fascist state. It will be a different kind of fascist state from the one the Germans evolved. ... But in the final analysis, it's based on power and on the inability to put human goals and human conscience above the dictates of the state. Its origins can be traced in the tremendous war machine we've built since 1945, the "military-industrial complex" that Eisenhower vainly warned us about, which now dominates every aspect of our life. The power

> of the states and Congress has gradually been abandoned to the executive department, because of war conditions, and we've seen the creation of an arrogant, swollen bureaucratic complex totally unfettered by the checks and balances of the Constitution. In a very real and terrifying sense, our Government is the CIA and the Pentagon, with Congress reduced to a debating society. Of course ... we won't build Dachaus and Auschwitzes; the clever manipulation of the mass media is creating a concentration camp of the mind that promises to be far more effective in keeping the populace in line. ... The ... awesome power of the CIA and the defense establishment seem destined to seal the fate of the America I knew as a child and bring us into a new Orwellian world where the citizen exists for the state and where raw power justifies any and every immoral act. ... I'm afraid, based on my own experience, that fascism will come to America in the name of national security.

In his foreword to the latest important book on the Kennedy case, Harold Weisberg's *Oswald in New Orleans* (New York: Canyon Books, [1967]), Garrison adds that national security "usually refers to the security of the men who allowed" such a disaster to occur. "The greater threat to national security is the cynical concealment of such facts from the people. Behind the facade of earnest inquiry into the assassination is a thought control project in the best tradition of (Orwell's) *1984*."

Jim Garrison's political beliefs are explicitly and superbly libertarian; in answer to the *Playboy* interviewer, Garrison said:

> over the years, I guess I've developed a somewhat conservative attitude — in the traditional libertarian sense of conservatism, as opposed to the thumb-screw-and-rack conservatism of the paramilitary right — particularly in regard to the importance of the individual as opposed to the state and the individual's own responsibilities to humanity.

It has been clear for some time that Jim Garrison is a man of enormous courage, courage to stand up against the entire Establishment, officialdom and news media, in a field where well over twenty witnesses who could help shatter the official Warren Commission case have met mysterious deaths. But it turns out that he is a man of keen insight and high principle as well.

CHAPTER 32

Whose Violence?

Ever since the massive demonstration at the Pentagon on October 21, the growing anti-war movement in this country has escalated its confrontations with the police and, on occasion, with federal troops. The highly militant and turbulent demonstrations against Dean Rusk at the New York Hilton and at the Oakland Induction Center embody an important and dramatic shift in the strategy and tactics of the anti-war movement: in its phrase, it has shifted "From Protest to Resistance."

Many Americans have deplored and denounced the "violence" engaged in by the demonstrators. This is a curious and misplaced emphasis on *who* is committing the violence that we see and read about. The troops and the police are armed to the hilt, and they face groups of totally unarmed demonstrators; it is invariably the police and the troops who do the clubbing, the kicking, and, of course, the arresting and incarcerating. How come nobody protests *that* massive violence, against which the "violence" committed by the demonstrators is virtually non-existent?

It is a curious world we live in. Here is the U.S. government, engaging daily in massive and brutal violence against the far less armed people of Vietnam, against virtually the entire civilian population, including the old, the women and children, North and South. Why does not the American populace rise up to denounce *that* violence?

For the first time in history, the American authorities release — deadpan — pictures of our prisoners being systemically tortured by our puppet troops with American troops looking on benignly. These pictures have been widely distributed through the news media. Who protests? Who cares? No, instead American indignation centers on some bearded youngsters who sit in at the entrances of induction centers.

To fully explain this reaction requires someone more expert than I in psychopathology. But one reason is fairly clear: the American public has been conditioned to believe that if the *government* commits violence, it is not really violence. Therefore, it is only when private persons or groups commit violence that indignation wells up.

When government officials — be they federal, state, or local — do anything, they are apparently clothed in such sanctity, such holiness and adoration, that their actions are transmuted automatically into the virtuous, the good, and the noble. All we need do to correct this confusion and to take a hard and accurate look at the government, is simply to apply the same moral standards to the minions of government that we would apply to anyone else.

That alone would be enough to make everyone a libertarian, and to expose the fact that the great source of crime and violence in the world today is the institution of government.

CHAPTER 33

Devaluation

After three years of putting the English people unmercifully through the wringer of "austerity," of ever-more crippling taxes and governmental wage controls; after three years of protesting to everyone up and down the country that the pound sterling would never, never be devalued, and that austerity was necessary to "protect the pound," Prime Minister [James Harold] Wilson finally threw in the sponge. One Saturday morning the stunned British public awoke to find that their sacrifices had been in vain and that the pound was now devalued. The latest chapter in government's eternal "credibility gap" with a long-suffering public has been written.

Devaluation comes about when government arbitrarily overvalues the worth of the its currency in terms of other currencies or in terms of the one world money, gold. For decades, Great Britain has been inflating its currency; i.e., pumping more pounds and bank claims to pounds into circulation, all done by the British government which, like all other governments in the modern world, has absolute control over the nation's monetary and banking system. And when more pounds are pumped into the economy, the true value of each pound — whether in terms of goods, other currencies, or gold — goes down. But the British government stubbornly clung to the increasingly overvalued price which it had set on the pound; hence claims to pounds in other countries piled up, and gold kept flowing out. Finally, after much travail for the British public, the government was forced to recognize the hard facts of reality: that the pound wasn't really worth $2.80 any longer. Hence, devaluation — the grudging acceptance of reality.

But, typically, the devaluation was puny: only 14 percent, and it looks as if the pound is still overvalued; so the austerity measure continue, as the British public is again told that it must buckle under to protect the new artificial value of the pound. Chances are good for another forced devaluation soon.

The lesson for the American public is all too clear. For the dollar, too, has been overvalued for years. The dollar has been continually inflated by the U.S. government until it is absurd to believe that it is still worth the 1933 price of $35 an ounce of gold. America, then, has also been losing gold steadily in the last decade, and its foreign economic policy has been devoted largely to persuading or intimidating foreign countries into *not* cashing in their huge dollar claims for gold, even though we have pledged to redeem them. All sorts of gimmicks, international pools and drawing rights, etc., have been concocted by the U.S. money managers in a desperate attempt to stave off the inevitable.

That inevitable is for *us* to accept reality, and that acceptance, which will surely come, and soon, is devaluation of the dollar — perhaps to $70 an ounce. That is the solution advocated by de Gaulle's brilliant monetary adviser, libertarian economic Jacques Rueff, and that is the solution which, after great fuss and feathers, will have to be employed.

But, once again, it is a solution that will come in the middle of some weekend night, and Americans will wake up to find that their government managers have lied to them time and time again. The "never, never" for devaluation of the dollar will go the way of all other such promises in the past. You can bet, however, that there will be no devaluation until the 1968 elections; for that is all Johnson would need to reduce his voting strength to virtually zero.

CHAPTER 34

Exchange Controls

Most economists have thought that "It Couldn't Happen Here" — not, in mighty America, the home of high productivity and, therefore, the home of free international trade. But is has happened, and because of the chronic inflationary policies of the U.S. government, we are now boxed into a situation where the administration has adopted that despotic and tyrannical method of rule hitherto confined to despised backward countries: exchange control.

Exchange control means that the dollar is so weak compared to its official price that gold flows continually out of the country, and to stop that flow of gold, nations resort to arbitrary decrees rationing the short supply of gold and foreign exchange, and prohibiting nations from spending their money abroad.

President Lyndon Johnson, in a New Year's gift to the American people, has instituted just such control, heralding an accelerating crackdown on American investments and travel abroad. This kind of direct interference with the way in which you or I wish to spend our money is not only patently unconstitutional, if the term has any meaning, it is also the final step toward a totalitarian economy. By what right does this man presume to dictate to supposedly free Americans where they can spend or invest their property?

Apart from being immoral, dictatorial, and unconstitutional, these exchange controls, though they will get ever tougher in coming months, will not and cannot work. In short, they will accomplish nothing in reducing the chronic deficit in the American balance of payments. For instance, suppose Americans reduce investment and spending abroad by $1 billion, as a result of the threats and outright coercion of the administration. Johnson and his Keynesian advisers automatically assume that our deficit will therefore be cut by that $1 billion. But it's not so, because this simply means that Europeans will have $1 billion less to buy our products, so that the flow of money into the U.S. will decrease by about the same amount. None of these frantic and despotic decrees will work.

In fact, trying to end the deficit by preventing people from spending their own money is like busting a thermometer to lower a patient's fever. It is an attack on the symptoms, rather than the causes. Our Brain Trusters in Washington never bother to ask: *Why* have we had this chronic deficit for the last two decades? Surely it is not from a sudden excess of greed or propensity to spend on the part of the American people. No, the reason is that the dollar, at the price we have pegged gold for over thirty years ($35 an ounce) is increasingly overvalued as more and more inflated dollars are poured into the economy by the government. At this arbitrary value, gold will flow out of the country, as people rush to dump dollars and buy gold and other foreign currency.

The solution in the short run is to devalue the dollar to a more realistic gold price (say, $70 an ounce). The solution in the long run is to stop the chronic American inflation. Eventually devaluation must come; it is inevitable. But, just as Mr. Wilson put the British people through three years of unnecessary sacrifice and torture to "save" an inflated pound, so Mr. Johnson is already beginning to call on all of us to "sacrifice" for the same futile and preposterous cause.

CHAPTER 35

The Coming American Fascism

For at least two decades we have been living in a society that has taken on all the characteristics of fascism. At home we have the fascist corporate state economy: an economy of monopolies, subsidies, and privileges run by a tripartite coalition of Big Business, Big Unions, and Big Government; and we have a military garrison state, with permanent conscription, tied to a permanent war economy fueled by armament contracts. We have an effectively state-owned or at best state-run educational system, from lower to higher, imbuing its charges with the glories of our government and our system, and training them to become cogs in the military-industrial-bureaucratic complex we have become.

In foreign affairs we have expanded all over the globe, grabbing bases and running governments everywhere, all in the name of a global crusade against the "international Communist conspiracy."

So far, then, we have duplicated fascism right across the board — except in one vital detail: We have not yet cracked down, except marginally, on freedom of speech and freedom of dissent in this country. But now the signs are ominously piling up that this particular and crucial aspect of freedom might be going down the statist drain. For the government is beginning what appears to be a massive crackdown on the growing anti-war movement — probably because it could tolerate this form of dissent only as long as it remained confined to the fringes of society. But now that the anti-war movement has been growing by leaps and bounds in numbers and in militancy, in breadth and in depth; now the government seems to be getting ready to revive the repressions on dissent which were rampant in the early stages of the Cold War.

There are many indications of this crackdown, from General Hershey's threat to use the draft to punish opposition by anti-war students, to the army's conviction of two anti-war activists near Ft. Sill, Oklahoma, for "trespassing on government property." But three leading instances will suffice here. First, Walter Teague and Mike Gimbel, two officers of the U.S. Committee to Aid the National Liberation Front of South Vietnam, after being beaten by police during the anti-draft demonstrations in New York last December, were indicted for outrageously severe charges; such that Teague, if convicted, faces up to fifteen years in jail, while Gimbel, against whom the charge is mere *possession* of a bottle of explosive powder, faces up to seven years in prison!

Secondly, the militant black nationalist writer LeRoi Jones, arrested and accused of *possessing* two revolvers, was convicted for this alleged crime and condemned to three years in prison without possibility of probation. Even if the charge is not a frameup, why should *possession* of a weapon make one a criminal? Is it not everyone's property right, as well as his constitutional right, to bear arms? But neither liberty nor property are the concern of those out to savage LeRoi Jones, and their true motives are revealed in the judge's bothering to read aloud, when making his decision, from Jones' poems, which are hardly related to his possessing a weapon. So now judges are literary critics, too!

The third, and most noteworthy, crackdown is the Justice Department's decision to indict, for possible long jail sentences, on the charge of exercising freedom of speech — counseling people to resist the draft — several leading figures in the anti-war movement, including Dr. Benjamin Spock and Yale Chaplain Rev. William Sloan Coffin. But good may emerge from this move toward fascism's last stage. We might see the courts declare the draft unconstitutional, as it surely is under the 13th Amendment's outlawry of involuntary servitude. At any rate, I predict we are going to see the anti-war movement do the reverse of the early Cold War movement's folding up and quitting — this movement is much too principled and determined for that.

CHAPTER 36

The Pueblo *Caper*

A remarkable thing has happened: Let the *Pueblo* be seized by North Korea, and every man-on-the-street becomes an international law "expert." "An outrage!" "An act of piracy!" "Nothing like this has happened since 1815!" The air is filled with declamations on the law of the sea; I expect at any time to hark back to the eighteenth century and find the press teeming with discussions of the law of capture, contraband theory, and how many puffs at the hornpipe are required for a party to board ship.

The first point one finds striking is the sudden devotion of American politicians to rules of international law, after America has violated it time and again, and consistently in Vietnam for several years, and after releasing pictures showing American soldiers aiding and supervising torture of prisoners in Vietnam. The stench of hypocrisy in this affair is overwhelming.

Even on the narrow point of the capture of the *Pueblo*, there are enough fuzzy areas and ambiguities to give pause to even the most hopped-up patriot. North Korea, like many nations of the "free world," claims twelve miles offshore as its territorial waters. The U.S. claims that the *Pueblo* was accosted sixteen miles out; the North Koreans said that the ship — which all sides acknowledge to have been a spy ship, pure and simple — was eight miles offshore. Four miles at sea seem to be pretty flimsy grounds for launching World War III.

And for those four flimsy miles, we are forced to rely on the word of a government which, as the astute and witty columnist Murray Kempton has reminded us, has consistently lied, and lied mightily, to the American people: during the U-2 incident, the Bay of Pigs, and now, it seems, at the Gulf of Tonkin, that mysterious incident in October, 1964 which served as the groundwork for all the escalation of the Vietnam war that the Johnson Administration has waged ever since. The American story about Tonkin has been changing steadily for years: At first a massive attack by North Vietnam's PT boats hurling numerous torpedoes at innocent American ships, the story has now been whittled down to one lone torpedo — maybe — against ships which admittedly had zig-zagged inside North Vietnamese territorial waters. But of course truth never really does catch up, in the public mind, with the Big Lie. Kempton concludes that, in this dispute, he is at this point forced to believe the North Koreans since *they* have not been lying to him lately.

With the advent of the *Pueblo* crisis, the air of Congress was filled with the predictable cries of the addled war hawks. Several joined Governor Reagan in calling, in the best John Wayne fashion, for an American fleet to go steaming up Wonsan Harbor to rescue ship and crew; one of the many difficulties, of course, is that the crew has long since been removed inland. Other statesmen want to bomb the ship to smithereens; apparently it makes no difference whether we rescue the ship or blow it up — so long as there is *some* mighty act of American violence. Meanwhile, we face the fact that, apart from one airborne division at Fort Bragg, N.C., there are no troops left with which to launch another war in Korea. As a result, some politicians are calling for the ultimate atrocity: atomic weapons. For this suggestion we can thank Senators [Henry M. "Scoop"] Jackson (D., Wash.) and [Strom] Thurmond (R., S.C.). Are we to blow up the Korean people, the ship and crew, and maybe the whole U.S. as well, over four disputed miles in the waters off Wonsan?

CHAPTER 37

The State of the War

As I write, the news comes that the Viet Cong (the Army of National Liberation of South Vietnam) has won its mightiest victory of the war. After suddenly, simultaneously, and successfully invading seven of the leading cities of South Vietnam (and the cities are the last strongholds of pro-U.S. forces), the V.C. have invaded Saigon itself, even unto the heart of the American embassy.

This crucial incident highlights an important fact of the war which until now has been carefully kept from the American people by their rulers in Washington. The U.S. has been in the Vietnam war in force since the spring of 1965. In Vietnam there is a wet season, stretching from about May to November, and a dry season, from November to May. Typically, all the great U.S. offensives have taken place upon the beginning of each dry season, as the U.S. forces have launched Operation This, That, and the Other, with various plans to establish interior forts, coastal enclaves, to "hold and clear," or to "search and destroy." At the beginning of every dry season, the U.S. has launched these offensives with a great deal of fanfare, claiming that now indeed the war is almost won, that now the tide has turned, etc.

There has been good reason for the Americans to exult as each dry season was reached, for the dry season alone permits the U.S. to use its spheres of advantage to the uttermost. In the wet season the U.S. planes cannot fly, and the U.S. tanks and heavy armored equipment sink into the mud.

Such was the pattern at the start of the dry seasons of 1965–66 and 1966–67, followed eventually by a petering out of the offensive, and the renewal of hope and promise the following year. But now, in this dry season, the pattern is very, very different. For with the coming of the dry season of 1967–68, the Viet Cong, for the first time, totally and irreversibly has the strategic and the tactical initiative. Now it is the V.C. that does the attacking, and the American forces that supply the heroic defense. The dramatic raids and invasions of the major cities by the V.C. are only the climactic demonstration of the vital fact that the war has indeed turned and turned completely.

For what this means is that the Viet Cong have the permanent initiative in the war. It means that the United States, despite its almost 600,000 troops in Vietnam (the vast bulk of its army) and despite the 700,000 and more Saigon puppet troops, has inevitably and ineluctably, lost the war. Short of destroying the country altogether, we cannot win. And now we are steadily losing, and losing with little more than 50,000 North Vietnamese troops in the country to aid their brethren of the South. If we commit the supreme folly of a land invasion of North Vietnam, we will have on our hands not only the current forces that are whipping us, but also 400,000 more men of the crack North Korean army, plus North Korean guerrillas, to say nothing of the Chinese.

Perhaps those who are not convinced of the immorality of the war in Vietnam will now be convinced of its total folly.

CHAPTER 38

The Garbage Strike

For nine days the garbagemen of New York City were out on strike, and the streets were piled high with putrefying mounds of garbage. The press and the public have been infuriated by the strike but, as in so many matters, the fury has been sadly misplaced. Government actions, backed by the public, have been the wrong war at the wrong place at the wrong time.

In the first place, Mayor John Lindsay stubbornly refused to accept the offer of the state mediation panel, and instead called on the governor to call out the National Guard to take on the duties of hauling and dumping the city's garbage. There are several things very wrong about this procedure. First, the amount of money it takes to call up the National Guard would cost the New York City taxpayers twice as much *per day* ($500,000) as it would cost *per year* if the mayor accepted the ;mediation offer as compared to the amount for which the mayor is holding out. Second, the National Guard is not very competent in garbage disposal, especially in operating garbage scows and cranes and incinerators. In short, you can't move garbage with bayonets.

He says it's a matter of "principle." First, the city should not give in to "blackmail," and second, the sanitation union is violating the state's Taylor Law, which outlaws strikes by public employee unions. Because of this law, Lindsay acted swiftly to put the head of the union, John Delury, in jail. But he soon found that jail doesn't move garbage either. And so, the violence against DeLury having failed abysmally, Lindsay proposed to escalate that violence by putting the National Guard into action — against which labor threatened a general strike throughout the city. The high "principle," then, turns out to be a despotic law violating everyone's inalienable right to strike; that is, to quit working — especially since there was no contract in force. Any law invading the right to strike comes close to being a slave-labor law.

So, within the context of the situation, Governor [Nelson]Rockefeller was perfectly sound in looking for mediation and in wanting to end the strike as quickly as possible and to get the garbage moving again. Lindsay's actions turned out to be petulant, hysterical, and despotic; and yet, Lindsay's position was backed fully by all the press of New York and by most of the public, which contented themselves with empty vituperation against the sanitation union.

In the broader sense, of course, the main problem is that the entire society has put itself at the mercy of labor unions, by passing laws privileging these unions and making them quasi-compulsory and, further, by accepting as some God-given rule the idea that no strike may be broken; in short, that it is unthinkable to simply fire strikers and hire replacements.

Thus, Mayor Lindsay would much rather jail union leaders than simply fire them and hire others in their place. For the corollary of the right to strike, which should be inviolable, is the right to fire strikers and to hire those who are willing to work at terms offered by the employers.

CHAPTER 39

The Vietnam Crisis

The Johnson administration is sinking every deeper into its quagmire of lies about the war in Vietnam. Now, as these lies come into ever greater confrontation with reality, they are becoming more openly ludicrous. Is there anyone left who really believes that the latest phase of remarkable Viet Cong victories represents the "last convulsive gasp" of the virtually defeated enemy? If it has done nothing else, the administration has added a great new law to military strategy: the more you're being defeated, the more this simply means that the enemy is becoming "desperate." The more you lose, the closer you come to "winning." How many more such "victories" can we stand?

Recently I wrote that the crucial new fact about the war in Vietnam is that the VC has permanently seized the strategic and tactical initiative in the war, an initiative which we had had during the previous dry seasons (approximately November to May), and which the Viet Cong had now obtained. But even I underestimated the swiftness and the force with which the VC would seize and push that initiative; even I underestimated the extent to which the VC is now winning the war.

The last stronghold of the U.S. and Saigon puppet forces had been the cities, and now they are strongholds no longer. For the VC launched a phenomenal simultaneous attack against seventy South Vietnamese cities — including thirty-five of the forty provincial capitals in the country. The VC still holds part of many of these cities, including Saigon and Hue, the largest. This means that they will remain there permanently, and that now we are permanently faced — short of wiping out the entire urban Vietnamese population, people we are supposedly fighting to "defend" — with guerrilla warfare in the urban as well as the rural areas.

The success of the VC in storming the cities reflects their overwhelming support among even the Saigonese and urban population, and the overwhelming public defection from the Saigon puppet regime. For how did the VC suddenly manage to pop up in the cities? By sneaking arms and equipment in among the civilian population in advance, and then walking into the cities in civilian guise. This can only be done with the overwhelming support of the population that aids you and secretes your arms in advance.

The VC also succeeded in capturing and raiding all the major South Vietnamese arsenals, and has won mass desertions from the Saigon army. Whole battalions of Saigonese troops have either returned to their home villages or have gone over in a body to the VC. How else can one explain the fact that U.S. infantry was needed to hold onto Saigon itself?

There are no safe areas whatever for American troops in Vietnam; there is no safe military rear area; the front is everywhere, and we are losing rapidly. We had best get out, and get out fast. If General [William] Westmoreland leaves the 6,000 American troops isolated and surrounded — by about 30,000 men — at the northwest outpost of Khe Sanh, we will probably get another Dien Bien Phu, and such a massacre will accelerate the getting-out process.

CHAPTER 40

The Escalation of Lyndon Johnson

The always perceptive *Wall Street Journal* recently printed a chilling report on the mood of Lyndon Johnson and the White House staff. While the administration promises up and down — even including the Hitlerian tactic of getting written guarantees from his generals — that Khe Sanh will hold, privately they are beginning to concede that Khe Sanh might well fall to the Viet Cong. The parallels between the 6,000 Marines trapped and surrounded at Khe Sanh and the 15,000 French troops trapped and captured at Dien Bien Phu fourteen years ago, are too numerous and too close to overlook. The disastrous strong-point strategy; the surrounding by a vast majority of enemy troops; the bombardment by artillery; the reliance on airlifts to supply the beleaguered troops; the inability even to secure the airfields; even the famous enemy tunnels and trenches which bring enemy fire up to the perimeter of the fortress; all these suggest the same inevitable conclusion.

The chilling thing is that administration officials are beginning — privately — to concede that Khe Sanh might well fall to the VC. But, they are beginning to reason in the increasingly mad logic of this administration, this might not be such a bad thing in the long run. For a massacre at Khe Sanh would mobilize and unify the American people behind the Vietnam War, and would permit the president to escalate that war still further: to go to Congress for a declaration of war on North Vietnam, for greater mobilization of bombers and land troops, and, last but not least, for the imposition of censorship and the ruthless cracking down upon free expressions of dissent within the United States.

If, indeed, this is the calculation of this administration, then we are in for a rough time over the next several months. But Johnson may be miscalculating — not about the probable fall of Khe Sanh, but over the mood of the American people. Historically, the American people can be hysterically stampeded into war at the sudden *beginning* of a conflict; stampeded by their rulers, who are anxious to expand their power and might, at home and abroad. This is what happened in the Spanish-American War ("Remember the *Maine*!"), World War I (the *Lusitania* sinking), and World War II (Pearl Harbor). But let a war drag on for years and let the American public get adjusted to the continuing drain of a protracted conflict, and its increasing war-weariness and disgust cannot be overcome by rage at sudden disasters. It's too late for that.

Meanwhile, in Vietnam, the VC continue their winning course. The permanent result of the VC offensive in the cities is as important as the drama and psychological gains of the offensive itself. For the Viet Cong are now firmly entrenched on the borders and outskirts of every city and every American military base in Vietnam, and they can shell and lob mortars into these areas at will; they can shift their attack and concentrate at will. In a deeper sense, every American enclave in Vietnam is now another Khe Sanh.

CHAPTER 41

The Amateur "Ideal"

This is an Olympic year and, like every Olympic year, it is a good time to contemplate the curious relic of "amateurism" that threatens to wreck every Olympics and many sporting events. At the Winter Olympics in Grenoble there was, and still remains, a recurring threat to disrupt and wreck the games on the altar of the amateur "ideal"; for a while the Olympic authorities almost ruined the ski events by insisting that the players wax over the names of the ski manufacturers, and now there is talk of robbing the great Jean-Claude Killy of his skiing medals because he might have accepted money for appearing in a photograph.

The phony amateurism ideal is based on the aristocratic, pre-capitalist theory that there is something wicked and evil, something tainted, about accepting money on the market for an expenditure of one's efforts and one's talents. And that there is something holy, pure, and noble about refusing to earn money for expending one's talents. This is a hangover from the old sneering by the feudal nobility and the court at engaging in trade or in business; at earning money for one's ability on the free market.

There is no question about the fact that the amateur principle is unrealistic; hence, all the evasions and short-circuiting of the amateur principle, and endless squabbles about how much non-athletic work an athlete must do for the corporation or organization that hires him before he can qualify as a simon-pure "amateur."

It is possible that the quality of American tennis might be saved because, at long last, amateur and professional tennis players will be allowed to participate in some of the same tournaments, a battle that was won in golf long ago.

There is no question that scuttling the amateur concept is the wave of the future, and that someday the distinction between amateur and professional will be dead as the dodo. But the point is that we should cease to regard octogenarian Avery Brundage and his fellow last-ditch champions of amateurism as battlers for the noble ideal; amateurism is a feudal remnant, a moral slap-in-the-face at everyone who earns his living honestly, and to the best of his abilities, on the free market.

It should be repudiated not only as unrealistic, but as pernicious and the opposite of an "ideal."

CHAPTER 42

What Does the Viet Cong Want?

How is it that the overwhelming majority of the people of South Vietnam support the National Liberation Front, the "Viet Cong"? A look into this question will help Americans who are bewildered at seeing so much of the world's population supporting what we simply regard as "Communist totalitarianism." If it were as simple as that, the Communists would find precious little support, and precious few members.

It is no coincidence that the mighty drive of 1967–68, which has established the Viet Cong in the position of winning the protracted war, was preceded by the adoption of an extremely important new political program; a statement of policy for the present and future NLF regime in South Vietnam. The policy statement was adopted last September 1, and was reprinted in full in the *New York Times* of December 15.

First, we should realize that the NLF are not simply communists, but a broad national coalition of numerous groups, including Buddhists, Catholic abbés, and middle-class parties; and in this coalition the communists play a leading role. Secondly, as a witness to this broad coalition, there is not a word in this lengthy political program about the establishment of a socialist society. On the contrary, the NLF platform is no more socialistic than those of the Democratic or Republican parties in the United States — and maybe a good deal less. Not only that: the major thrust of the program is the guarantee of the private property of business and especially of the peasantry, who are the vast bulk of the Vietnamese population. In addition, the program proclaims and guarantees the freedom of religion, of national minorities to have their own language and autonomy, and of speech, press, assembly, association, demonstrations, and forming of political parties, as well as "inviolability of the human person," freedom of residence and movement, and the secrecy of the mails.

On property rights, the NLF program promises "to protect the right to ownership of the means of production and other property of the citizens." It adds that "the state will encourage the capitalists in industry and trade to help develop industry, small industries and handicrafts," and will "give due consideration to the interests of small traders and small manufacturers." Above all, the program repeatedly guarantees the right of peasants to their land, and promises to turn over any lands confiscated by the state (e.g., the "lands of the U.S. imperialists") to the peasantry.

There are other important aspects of the NLF program which have won due attention from the press, such as guarantees of equal treatment to defecting troops and a pledge of a foreign policy of peace and neutrality. But in the long run, the guarantees to private capitalist and especially to peasant property are the most important, for these guarantees, set against the anti-peasant policies of the Saigon puppet regime, go a long way to account for the puzzling fact that the undeveloped countries of the world tend to support communists rather than the United States. It is because the communists proclaim their support for national independence and for the private property of the peasantry, while the U.S. invariably backs colonial and feudal landlord regimes that are hated throughout these countries.

CHAPTER 43

April Fool Week

The fantastic, incredible, shattering events of April Fool Week came with such bewildering speed that it's almost impossible to sort them out and analyze them at this early date. We pundits and columnists were taken by surprise almost every day, and many of us formed brilliant theories one day, only to see them shattered by the onrushing and changing facts of the day following. The three mighty events that week were, of course, the unbelievable withdrawal of President Johnson on April Fool Eve, the agreement of Hanoi to begin preliminary peace talks, and the assassination of Martin Luther King. Let us set aside the King murder and its implications for later analysis, and concentrate now on Johnson and Vietnam.

The first point we must make is to protest vigorously at the mighty wave of adulation that swept over the man who, up to the end of March, was the most universally hated president in many generations. Let us hear no more of the sickening claptrap about Johnson's noble and Christ-like act of self-sacrifice, his self-immolation for the unity of the nation, and all the rest of the hogwash. I half-expected some of the Democratic Party hacks who led in the hosannahs to proclaim that LBJ had "died for our sins." Lyndon Johnson withdrew because, indeed, he had gravely "divided" the nation, but the division was all his doing, the doing of a man who had led this nation into an ever-escalating senseless and infamous war in Vietnam. He found himself, after three years of large-scale war, losing that war, amid a rising tide of dissent, opposition, and even hatred at home. Beset at every hand, losing at home and abroad, Johnson decided to get out while he had some shred of reputation left. It must be recognized that the main lesson of the Johnson withdrawal is *not* his unexpected nobility; and saintliness, but the fact that the rising and swelling tide of the anti-war movement, the growing mass sentiment of determined opposition to the war and the draft, has won a tremendous victory: the anti-war movement — along with the remarkable fighting spirit of the Vietnamese people — was able to bring down the mightiest and most powerful man in the world: the President of the United States. It was a fantastic victory for mass public pressure from below — a pressure both at home and in Vietnam — that unexpectedly bubbled through the hard crust of Establishment rule and orthodox political party structures, to make itself heard and felt on the American political scene.

It was a victory of concerned private persons against the most powerful ruling machine in the world today. It was a demonstration that individual persons who believe and feel deeply enough about the sins of the government, and act upon that belief, *can* have an impact, even unto the toppling of the mighty head of that governmental Leviathan. This great victory can never be taken away from the people of this country.

Even recognizing this victory, however, it behooves us to remain on our guard. We cannot trust Mr. Johnson, as has been shown an almost infinite number of times in the past, and we cannot believe that he was not trying, in his desperation, to "pull a Nasser": to resign dramatically and then have the mass of the people, in a wave of frenzied sentimentality, bear him aloft and "force" him to continue in office. We cannot be sure that Johnson was not, and to this day is still not, hankering after a "draft." Fortunately, the massive sympathy vote that many pundits expected in the Wisconsin primary did not materialize; and who knows what "draft" sentiment might have been whipped up if Johnson had won in Wisconsin? But Johnson lost handily, and that menace is over; but we must still be on our guard for another opportunity to whip up a sentimental massive turn to renominate President Johnson.

Liberty depends upon eternal vigilance.

CHAPTER 44

Martin Luther King

Okay. I deplore and condemn the murder of the Rev. Martin Luther King, Jr. But no more and no less than I deplore and condemn any murder of any man. The attention and the *brouhaha* being paid to the King murder is more than a little ridiculous and more than a little revolting.

Every day tens of thousands of people are murdered, and nobody gives a hoot; no flags at half mast, no stores and banks and ball games close down for close to a week. When the great black leader, Malcolm X was assassinated no banks and no schools shut down, and no vice president appeared at his funeral. It appears to me that there is more fuss and feathers about the assassination of the Rev. King than there was about the assassination of President Kennedy — or at least as much.

Why? Why should this one murder and this one funeral command the continuing and uninterrupted attention of the entire nation? The civil rights movement is opposed to discrimination, and yet to single our Dr. King's funeral for sole and unremitting attention appears to me an insult and discrimination against all other victims of murder and foul play, here and throughout the world.

I have a goodly hunch about the answer to this mystery, and the answer makes the whole spectacle repellent and shameful and hypocritical, and not simply ridiculous. I have a hunch about why department store after department store took out black-bordered ads with Dr. King's portrait, proclaiming that they would shut down in honor of his funeral. The hunch: that these worthies acted not out of grief and respect, but out of pure fear. Fear that unless continual low obeisance is made in the direction of the Rev. King, the Negroes of this nation would rise up and level them to the ground. In a sense, these stores and schools were paying a kind of anticipatory blackmail. It's a truly degrading spectacle. So intensely did this fear grip midtown Manhattan on the Friday after the murder that firm after firm released its employees early, in response to wild rumors that permeated New York that the whole of midtown Manhattan was in flames and ruins. Invariably, these employees rushed home and barricaded their doors, waiting for the holocaust that never came.

Rev. King, far and away the Number One leader of the Negro people, was also its leading apostle of absolute non-violence; hence he was the major restraining force on the developing Negro revolution. All the more was this true because, in moments of crisis, he relaxed his absolute non-violence to come out in favor of the use of violence by federal troops to put down Negro rioting — as he did in Watts three years ago, and as he did in last summer's urban rebellions. Now that influence is gone; like Gandhi, his mentor in non-violence mass movements, he was cut down by an assassin's bullet.

Perhaps the most important sign of radicalizing of the Negro mood in the wake of Dr. King's death was the extensive rioting in Washington, D.C. For the Negroes of Washington had always been very quiet and docile, most of them being low-grade civil servants with a genteel status in the Negro community. But now Washington, for the first time, has erupted, and we were treated to the highly revealing picture of soldiers with machine guns on the White House steps. The veil, the mask, the illusion that the government rules by voluntary "consent" of the public was, in those photographs and in that reality, stripped away, and we saw clearly, some for the first time, that the government rules, in the last analysis, by the gun and the bayonet — and by these alone.

CHAPTER 45

All the Withdrawals

President Johnson's withdrawal from the presidential race is the last of a series of withdrawals that caught the mass media totally and completely be surprise: Governor [George] Romney's sudden pullout while campaigning in New Hampshire, and Governor [Nelson] Rockefeller's decision to withdraw from the race after all his friends and associates were assured that he would enter. In every case, the withdrawer proclaimed the reason to be his desire to "unify" the party and/or the country.

All this gives me an idea. If these withdrawals are so beneficial for the party and for the country, why shouldn't more politicians and potential candidates follow the noble example set by these idealistic men? Why shouldn't *everyone* withdraw: Nixon, [Robert F.] Kennedy, McCarthy, Humphrey, or whoever? As each politico withdraws, we can all strew their paths with flowers and hail their nobility and self-sacrifice. It would then be a shame and a disgrace for anyone to run for the presidential office; and *anyone* who dared to do so would be a kind of moral leper in the community. Of course, the result of this onrush of morality in the land would be that there would be no one available to run for the presidency, and I'm afraid that the result would be that the august office of the presidency would be declared vacant.

With the presidency vacant for four years, there would be no one to make war, no one to submit a federal budget, no one to urge Congress to pass new legislation, no one to execute the laws, no one to push us all around. Perhaps after the initial shock, we would all find ourselves immeasurably freer and happier than we were before.

Then a clamor would well up to extend the benefits of this moratorium on public office even further, and all sorts of bureaucrats and politicians, high, low, and middling, would resign or refuse to run for office. Government offices would become vacant across the length and breadth of the land, and joy would reign unconfined. For anyone to run or to accept any public office would be considered a moral and an aesthetic disgrace, to be shunned by one and all.

One office I would like to see mass resignations from, pronto, is membership on one's friendly local draft board. The draft board members perform their noble service unpaid; yet, just as charity is supposed to be silent, so these worthies get upset if their names become known to the public that suffers its sons torn away at their beck and call. Let us find out who our friendly local draft board members are, and let us not forget them when we cast our moral opprobrium at the politicians and bureaucrats.

CHAPTER 46

The Peace Negotiations

Lyndon Johnson's April Fool peace offensive was, as Senator [William J.] Fulbright had the enormous courage to point out, a phony. Hanoi had repeatedly said that it would not negotiate until the United States unconditionally and permanently halted the bombing of North Vietnam. Johnson's bombing announcement fooled many people into believing that this is what Johnson had decided to do; instead Johnson continued to bomb North Vietnam up to 200 miles north of the border and, in fact, he bombed this large zone much more intensely after the "bombing halt" than he had done before.

But Johnson had pulled an extraordinarily shrewd maneuver. In the wave of mass adulation and sentimentality over Johnson's withdrawal, the massive hatred and distrust of Johnson at home and abroad evaporated and changed to sympathy and pity; and in the course of this shift, Johnson managed to accrue to himself the mantle of peace. As the American press proclaimed, Hanoi was now on the spot; without doing anything really constructive, Johnson had managed to acquire the aura of peace here and throughout the world. And Johnson confidently expected that Hanoi would maintain its long-held position, and then become, in the eyes of Americans and of world opinion, a stubborn war-making nation. Johnson could then resume and re-escalate the war with impunity.

Not only that: by his brilliant maneuver, Mr. Johnson was, at one blow, able to co-opt the entire "peace" position of Messrs. [Robert F.] Kennedy and [Eugene] McCarthy, his dangerous rivals. In all the justifiable excitement about the McCarthy and Kennedy campaigns, and in the general hope that they offer significant alternatives to the war, an important point has been lost sight of: For all their sharp criticisms of the war, neither Kennedy nor McCarthy go beyond a call for stopping the bombing and negotiating with all parties, including the National Liberation Front of South Vietnam. Neither call for immediate withdrawal from Vietnam. As a result, Johnson's negotiation-and-bombing curtailment comes pretty close to the maximum demands of his rivals for the nomination. *If* Hanoi had refused to negotiate and Johnson had resumed full-scale war, Kennedy and McCarthy would have been hard put to resume their sharp attacks on the President's policies. By agreeing to negotiate, Hanoi has, with equal shrewdness, tossed the ball back to President Johnson, or at least, has taken any onus off its own shoulders.

Aside from all this, *will* these negotiations bring peace? And when? For if Johnson is able to conclude a full peace settlement by the end of August, it is again possible that his lieutenants will be able to engineer a "draft" by acclamation of the new peace-hero.

I am reasonably sure that this will not happen; that, if peace is concluded, it is still a long way off. The Korean negotiations took two years to conclude peace, and the parties now are at least as far apart as they were then.

CHAPTER 47

Shooting Looters

The great debate that raged during the post-King-funeral riots, and will continue to rage in the wave of ghetto rioting this summer, is: Should looters be shot?

Many defenders of property rights are backing the position of Chicago's Mayor Richard Daley that looters would be shot by the police, and are criticizing such officials as New York's Mayor John Lindsay, who maintains that his police will not shoot children for looting stores. The issue is being posed: the lives of the looters vs. the property rights of the merchants.

Those libertarians who favor maximum force to stop looting had best reconsider their position. Would they, for example, favor executing a young lad who steals an apple from a fruit stand? If not, why not? Are not property rights sacred?

The confusion here comes not from a disagreement on the right of the merchant to his property, but from an absence, among libertarians, of a well-thought-out theory of punishing invasions of that property right. Among those who have thought about this problem, there is a division of opinion; some libertarians oppose any use of force, even in self-defense. While I deeply respect this position, I do not agree with it. I believe that everyone has the right to use violence in defense of his property against invasion, but *only* in some kind of proportion to the crime itself. Any punishment must be limited to being proportionate to the crime; in the old phrase, "let the punishment fit the crime." Therefore, if a man is attacked by a criminal and his life is in danger, he has, in my view, a perfect right to defend himself by any means necessary, up to and including the killing of the attacker. But if a merchant sees a kid running off with his apple, he has no right whatever to shoot that kid, because that would be tantamount to capital punishment for a minor property offense; the punishment would be grossly disproportionate, to such an extent that the merchant himself would then be an invader of the right of the looting kid to his own person and his own life. The merchant would then be an unjustified murderer.

Hence, the use of lethal weapons in self-defense, or in defense of others, is only morally justifiable if the victim's life is in danger. If it is not, then such excessive violence is in itself just as criminal and invasive of the looter's right to life as is any other capital crime.

Every man, then, has a moral right to his own property, which *includes*, and includes above all else, his property in his own person and life. When a man invades the property right of another, he only loses his own rights *to the extent* that he has invaded the similar right of his fellow man.

Therefore, shooting looters, whether by the merchant himself or by the police, is absolutely impermissible. The right to life, after all, *is* more important than the right to own a camera or a color TV set, as important as the latter undoubtedly are.

CHAPTER 48

The Revolutionary Mood

Anyone who has anything to do with the nation's campuses knows that the atmosphere has changed drastically over the last couple of years; even over the last few months. The signs are everywhere.

Take Harvard, for example. Until a few months ago, the mood of Harvard students was, and always had been, cautiously well-buttoned and moderate; Harvard students know that they make up the coming elite of the nation, and they comport themselves accordingly. Radical writings or ideas were entertained by only a small hippie minority on the campus. But now, the New York *Village Voice* reports from Harvard that, under the spur of the failing Vietnam War and the Federal government's decision to draft graduate students, an amazing shift has taken place on campus. *Everyone* is now radical, everyone not only deeply opposes the war and the draft, but talk of "resist," "defy," even "bomb" and "assassinate," fills the air. The point is not so much that Harvard students will be carrying out such deeds, but that general campus opinion has so radicalized that they can now openly support such previously "unthinkable" views. A phenomenal number of college students, at Harvard and elsewhere, are now seriously considering emigrating to Canada to avoid the draft.

At every campus, radicalizing is going on at great speed. Iona College at New Rochelle, New York, until now a highly conservative Catholic college whose only political club had been the right-wing Young Americans for Freedom, recently had a demonstration against napalm-making Dow Chemical Company which mobilized no less than two hundred students, and YAF could only collect five students for a counter-demonstration. An old friend of mine, a graduate student at the University of Chicago whose arguments against the draft have always been cautiously moderate, stressing the economic efficiency of a volunteer army, now talks only of emigrating to Canada, and he reports that throughout campuses in the Midwest, the same kind of change is going on.

Not only students but also faculty; it is almost impossible now to find any intellectual who either favors the war in Vietnam or who has anything but loathing for President Johnson. Everywhere, young faculty members who have previously cared nothing for politics, now passionately oppose the war.

But not only that: This opposition to the war and to the U.S. government has, in surprisingly many instances, deepened into opposition to all government whatsoever — into a truly libertarian insight into the nature of the state apparatus. What began as purely a revulsion against the war has now started to deepen into an all-out opposition to the state itself.

CHAPTER 49

The McCarthy Crusade

The presidential campaign of Senator Eugene McCarthy has tapped a great deal of enthusiasm among considerable segments of American life. Particularly is this true of the nation's campuses, for students and faculty alike. His lone courage in launching the race against overwhelming odds and against the displeasure of the President, combined with his opposition to the Vietnam war and his scholarly tone and style, have won the hearts of almost the entire American college community, as well as other middle-class Americans. Not only has he tapped rising opposition to the war, but his professorial and low-key qualities (he used to be a professor of political science) and his storybook victories have generated a personal commitment to McCarthy among surprising numbers of people.

Take a few portents: At Columbia University, members of the two highly conservative campus organizations, the Douglas MacArthur Club and the Conservative Union, have shifted to McCarthy. At the Polytechnic Institute of Brooklyn, with a student body so conservative that Goldwater won an overwhelming victory there in a straw poll in 1964, there is only one presidential campaign organization, and that is for Senator McCarthy. Innumerable conservative friends of mine have enlisted in the McCarthy movement, including some who until recently had been advocates of the war in Vietnam.

Yet, if we dig below the surface attractiveness of the McCarthy campaign, we find that there is precious little sound reason for all the enthusiasm. A critic of Johnson's Vietnam policies Senator McCarthy may be, but his position on Vietnam is not really that different; what he wants is *not* immediate withdrawal, but a halt in the bombing of North Vietnam, and negotiations with all parties, including the National Liberation Front. Now that President Johnson seems to have virtually adopted this position, there is little of fundamental criticism of the war that McCarthy can still offer. Furthermore, McCarthy is in favor of continuing the slavery of the draft; the furthest he has gone on that issue is to offer alternative slave-service instead of jail to draft-refugees who might decide to return from Canada.

For, in the last analysis, Senator McCarthy is not a libertarian to any extent, but a liberal, albeit a member of that wing of liberalism which is far more intelligent and sophisticated than the brute wing headed by President Johnson. McCarthy saw that the Vietnam war was hopeless for American imperialism, and favored phasing out, *not* because he is opposed to imperialism, but because he realistically sees that its cause there is hopeless and not worth continued warfare. This is a more intelligent and reasoned view than that of Johnson-Humphrey-Rostow, and it may well be better to have McCarthy in the White House than Johnson, but it is hardly a view that should send libertarians into gales of enthusiasm. Let us reserve our enthusiasm for better causes.

CHAPTER 50

Columbia: The Night of Infamy

On April 29, 1968, in the dead of a night that will live in infamy in the annals of education in this country, Columbia University President Grayson Kirk and Vice President David Truman ordered onto the campus 1,000 cops, who proceeded to club, pummel, and drag into paddy wagons 720 students and faculty, as well as to brutalize thousands of innocent onlookers. The students had occupied and sat-in at several buildings at Columbia for a week, an act of non-violent disobedience to dramatize their demands for Columbia to end its connection with the Vietnam War through the governmental Institute of Defense Analysis, to stop construction on a gymnasium in a public park against the protests of the local community, and to institute more power by students and faculty in the decisions of the university which is, after all, an academic community of teachers and students. The faculty members were lined up in front of the struck buildings to protect the students from any intrusion of police violence, so they were clubbed by the police to get to the demonstrators. Despite the frenzied brutality of the police, the demonstrators never actively resisted arrest; they were simply not very cooperative in the arresting process.

Whether one favors or opposes the sit-in tactics of the demonstrators, there is no excuse, no justification whatsoever, for the Columbia administration to call in a thousand cops to use violence against un-armed students. It is the height of irony that, shortly before their monstrous deed, Kirk and Truman, at a press conference, sharply criticized the striking students for "resorting to force"; in contrast, Kirk and Truman called upon the ancient academic verities of reason, peace, and the free search for truth. Then, boom! came the *polizei*, ordered in by those same men, who seemed to see no inconsistency with their previous pronouncements.

The student and faculty body at Columbia, and indeed elsewhere, learned many hard-won lessons that night. They learned that underneath the high-flown sentiments about reason and free inquiry in the academic community there lies the mailed fist. They learned that these same high-flown academic leaders refuse to negotiate one iota when a supposedly crucial "principle" (not giving amnesty to transgressors) is in danger. And so, while less eminent but far more sensible universities like Boston University and Long Island University quickly granted complete amnesty to *their* sit-in students the previous week, and had the whole episode under control and forgotten inside of twenty-four hours, the rulers of mighty Columbia refused to do the same and called out their police-hooligans instead. The students and the faculty learned that an institution that is happy to cooperate in research for napalming innocent peasants is hardly going to stop short at clubbing a thousand or so students.

This learning process will cost Columbia very dear. The martyred demonstrators, emerging bloody but unbowed from the buildings under police charge, held up the V-for-victory signal. For they knew that by losing this engagement they had won the war; throughout the campus, the majority of students and many of the faculty, previously apathetic or opposed to the strike, are now so deeply angered at the police (most of them learned about "police brutality" for the first time) and at the administration, that they're determined to throw the administration out and to strike until their demand is met. This is the way revolutions proceed: A small but determined group embarks on a dramatic deed to publicize its demands; they are met with brute violence by the power structure; this brings the rest of the subject population over to the revolutionary side. At Columbia, the revolution has begun.

CHAPTER 51

The Student Revolution

Recently I wrote in these columns of the accelerating revolutionary mood on the nation's campuses. It is now clear that I underestimated the scope and depth of the looming student rebellion: for that rebellion is not only occurring now on *American* campuses, but throughout the world. In the U.S., there have been countless student sit-ins, with the mightiest, of course, being the Columbia crisis, which succeeded in closing Columbia College for the rest of the semester: but even more important, student rebellions are coming close to toppling governments in Europe, especially in Poland, West Germany, and France.

The amazing events in France highlight the revolutionary process at work. Here has been France, chafing for over a decade of near-dictatorship by De Gaulle. Add to this the archaic, bureaucratic, state-ridden and state-owned educational system, and the ingredients were brewed for student rebellion. Just as in the smaller model at Columbia, the student rebellion began as a sit-in and demonstration by a relatively small group of militant student rebels. Just as at Columbia, the police, called in to force the demonstrators into line, clubbed and beat their way through the student protestors. The savage brutality inflicted on the students swung the French working class behind the students, just as at Columbia the brutality swung the host of moderate students behind the strike. Throughout France, the cry arose: "De Gaulle! Assasin!," the analog of Columbia's "Kirk Must Go!"

What do the students want? Obviously their aims are vague and ill-defined. But that is the way it always is in revolution; nobody sits down and draws up a blueprint of how the revolution should or will turn out. On the contrary, once launched the revolution proceeds on its own inner dynamic, and the revolutionaries become educated in the course of the struggle itself. But the students do know, and clearly, what it is they are *against*; they are against the present system, and specifically against the state-ridden educational bureaucracy endemic in the world today. They are, as it were, instinctive libertarians, lashing out in fury at institutions which they perceive are oppressing and manipulating them. One thing is certain: These kids are not "Communists." Take, for example, the case of "Red Rudi" Dutschke, the famous young leader of the West Berlin student rebels. Despite his nickname, Rudi found that he had to leave East Germany, where he was born, because he couldn't take the oppressive Communist system of his homeland. Also, as a Christian youth leader, Dutschke found that he was particularly disliked by the East German regime. The Communist Party invariably was very late in endorsing the current student rebellions — the French Party first subjected them to bitter attack — and only swung behind the demonstrations when it was all too clear that if the Communists did *not* back the students they would lose all hope of support in the coming generation.

It's true that the idols of the West German and the French youth, and the American rebels too, are such Communist leaders as Mao, Che Guevara, and Ho Chi Minh. But they are not revered as Communists; no one, after all, likes very much, let alone worships, such current Communist leaders at Brezhnev, Gomulka, or Gus Hall; the reason is that the above leaders are admired not as Communists, but as successful revolutionaries. In this modern, complex, and militarized world, Ho, Che, and Mao were able to make revolution; it is this achievement, not Communism, that leads the young to idolize them.

At any rate, I, for one, shall not weep for whatever might be swept away of the old, state-dominated, bureaucratic university structures. But, whether we like it or not, whether we cheer or deplore, hold on to your hats: The international student revolution has begun.

CHAPTER 52

Assassination — Left and Right

The tragic murder of Senator Robert Kennedy points up an interesting fact about all the recent assassinations and assassination attempts that has gone unnoticed: that every single murder or attempted murder was of a leader of what may broadly be called the "Left" — John Kennedy, Senator Kennedy, Malcolm X, "Red Rudi" Dutcshke, the West German student leader, Medgar Evers, and the Reverend Martin Luther King. How is it that among this spate of murders, no right-wing leader has been assassinated? None of the cliches, true though they may be, about America being a "violent society" resolves this peculiar problem.

In my view, the answer lies in a grave misunderstanding of the situation, Left and Right, each in its own camp. In short, what we have in the world is a State apparatus, run more or less "peacefully" and quietly, with more or less stability by a ruling elite or Establishment, with the exploited but torpid masses paying the bill. To overthrow this Old Order, or existing statist regime, which is broadly the task of the Left, requires charismatic and dynamic leaders to rouse the masses out of their torpor, to expose their exploitation by the ruling classes, and then to move to overthrow that rule.

Therefore, the Left, being in one or another sense revolutionary, requires dynamic individual leaders to promote that revolution. Hence, some intelligent members of the Right, those devoted to the status quo, realizing the great dependence of the Left on their leaders, particularly in the critical early stages of the revolution, move to assassinate those leaders and to nip the situation in the bud. The irony is that the Left doesn't realize the importance to it of such dynamic leaders and, therefore, does not move, in one way or another, to protect them. For the Left, naively believing that all of history is determined by broad social forces and classes of people, gravely underestimates the importance of individual leadership — its own leadership — in such a struggle. While it is true that individual leaders cannot make a revolution if the fertile soil is not there, inspired leadership to cultivate that soil is just as important. The Left, a prisoner of its own naive view of history, does not realize this.

On the other hand, the Left doesn't assassinate Right-wing leaders for the same reason: Since it is broad social forces rather than individual leaders that matter, what would be the point of killing Mr. X if Mr. Y, put in by the same existing system to replace him, is just as bad? Ironically, in *this* case, the Left is more nearly correct, for the job of running an existing Establishment — in contrast to the task of rousing the masses to overthrow it — is just about the same from one Establishment ruler to the next. Therefore, in the case of the *Right* wing, one leader is just about the same as the next.

Thus: Both sides, Left and Right, are far more correct in analyzing the role of leadership in the opposition than in their own camp.

CHAPTER 53

French Revolution — 1968

Whether it fizzles, as it seems finally to be doing, or triumphs, there are many lessons to be learned from the phenomenal month-long French Revolution of 1968. First, it gives the lie, once and for all, to the widespread myth that revolutions, whether or not desirable, are simply impossible in the modern, complex, highly technological world. When the mythologists were confronted with the Chinese, Vietnamese, Algerian, and Cuban revolutions, all clearly triumphant, they said: Oh, well, perhaps there can still be revolution in the underdeveloped countries, but *not* in the Western world. Then came the successful Hungarian Revolution of 1956 — successful until the Soviet re-invasion. The excuse then was that Oh, well, Hungary was still a largely rural and undeveloped country.

But now France, mighty France — cradle of the Western world, and birthplace of revolutions. France, a possessor of the H-bomb, stopped in its tracks and almost toppled by that famous revolutionary weapon never until now successfully used: the general strike. Modern, complex technology requires skilled people to work it, and if these people refuse to work, bingo, you have a revolutionary situation. So now we know and we will know forevermore, that revolution *is* possible in the developed Western world.

A second interesting item is what sparked the massive general strike — it was the same spark that ignited each and every ghetto rebellion in the

U.S. cities last summer: massive police brutality. As in Columbia University, the police brutality was directed against students, who were beaten, clubbed, gassed, and grenaded by the French police. The question: Why is it that in the U.S. most people were angry at the students and supported the police, while the reverse happened in France?

One answer to this puzzle is the very different attitude toward the cops in France. Every Frenchman, regardless of income and social class, has a deep, abiding hatred in his bosom of the police. For one reason, Frenchmen tend to be devoted to freedom of speech and demonstration, and they understand that it is always the police who invade that freedom; secondly, every Frenchman has had his teenage bust-up with the cops.

For it is a French tradition that when a Frenchman receives his coveted high-school diploma, he engages in a traditional cut-up called the "monomial"; and it is also traditional that the monomial is always busted up with great brutality by the police. So every Frenchman has a keen hatred of the police force nourished within him; hence the common French nickname for the police: not so much the well-known *flics*, or "cops," but *les cognes* (those who-hit-people). Cops, to the French, are those who go about hitting people, and when they did so in violation of a century-old tradition of no cops on the university campus, all of France exploded. Another important lesson is the counter-revolutionary role, probably the main reason for the revolution's ultimate defeat, played by the French Communist Party. The student rebels, who tend to be anarchists, correctly regard the Communist Party as a pillar of the existing Establishment. The Communists opposed the students from the beginning, then finally joining the bandwagon, then induced the workers to surrender their demands. All of France now knows what the New Left has been saying for years: that the Communist Party is a pillar of the "conservative" Establishment. If Americans began to absorb that fact, their view of the world would be far different from what it is today.

CHAPTER 54

Draft Boards

One of the most powerful forces in the system of conscription slavery in this country is also one of the most secret and least known: your friendly local draft board. Until very recently, the membership of each local board was shrouded in total secrecy. Even now, when official policy is at last to make the names public, it is virtually impossible to rout out the names from the Selective Service bureaucracy, and to answer such vital questions as: How are the draft boards selected? Who selects them? And on what criteria? Millions of kids have been drafted over the years, without having the slightest idea of *who* these draft board members, with virtual power of life and death over them, really are.

All this goes starkly against the official theory that draft board members are chosen among the local communities, among people who will know the special circumstances of the kids being drafted, and who could therefore act in accordance with their unique knowledge. The Selective Service literature itself says:

> The decentralized organization of the Selective Service System is ... designed as a convenience to all registrants, providing them with ready access to a personalized unit of the System. ... The unpaid board members are often the neighbors of the registrants. The decisions are based on a

> knowledge of local conditions and the circumstances surrounding each individual.

It all sounds very cozy; yet, in those cases that have been ferreted out by enterprising newsmen, it is the reverse of the truth. After a lengthy runaround, two "underground" New Left papers, the New York *Free Press* and the *Mid-Peninsula Observer* in California, have been able to get hold of and publicize the names of the draft board members in their areas. Almost uniformly, they found (1) that the draft board members did *not* live in the communities over which they rule; and (2) that low-income minority group youngsters were being drafted by high-income whites who lived far from their communities. Thus, in Manhattan over 88 percent of draft board members do *not* live in the communities they rule over; the chairman of the draft board for central Harlem, which drafts low-income Negro youths, lives in the wealthy white community of Great Neck, many miles away from Manhattan, on Long Island.

Little is known so far about these draft board members, although it is already clear that there is a high percentage of lawyers with political connections, and of local school district officials; in short, so-called grass roots people who are, in reality, tied in with the governmental apparatus. It also seems that vacancies in the boards are, in effect, filled by the remaining members themselves, thus making them a self-perpetuating little oligarchy.

One thing is strikingly clear: The draft board members are the willing mainstay of the entire Selective Service System; they not only lend their sanction to evil and to slavery, they are the chief operating arm of that enslavement. They have much blood to answer for. No wonder they want to operate in strict secrecy and anonymity! In its mendacious literature, the Selective Service System claims that "draft board members are frequently consulted (by potential draftees) at their homes or place of business." Let us hope that this pious hope will soon be a reality, and that these members will indeed begin to be consulted by their "clientele."

CHAPTER 55

Humphrey or Nixon: Is There Any Difference?

Campaign year 1968 is rapidly educating the American people to the futility and the undemocratic nature of the electoral process. For in the face of all the polls and other expressions of public opinion that reveal McCarthy and Rockefeller as by far the most popular of their respective parties, the party hacks who run the Democratic and Republican conventions are determined to nominate *their* choices: [Hubert H.] Humphrey and Nixon. This blatant flaunting of the will of the oligarchy in the face of popular choice shall not be forgotten this time; and many millions will become permanently disenchanted with the entire American political process.

It is also more evident than ever before that there is hardly a smidgin of difference between the two major party candidates. Both Humphrey and Nixon are pre-eminently the spokesmen of hawkishness and aggression abroad and of the welfare-warfare corporate state at home: Both want to continue the New Deal-Fair Deal and both want to combine the carrot of federal funds with the stick of armed suppression to deal with the urban ghettoes. The fact that Humphrey's rhetoric is slightly more progressive-statist and Nixon's more conservative-statist is purely a function of their respective constituencies within the broad Corporate State consensus. The difference is purely that: a matter of rhetoric only.

And yet the disquieting thing is that Nixon, over the years, has shown the ability to attract a number of people who even call themselves "libertarians."

I remember well the campaign of 1960, when a whole slew of my friends and acquaintances, many self-styled "libertarians," began popping up in the Nixon camp, some high among his staff of advisers. Their story was always the same: "Privately, Dick really agrees with us; he told me this many times. ..." Etcetera. What malarkey! Why didn't these fools realize that being all things to all men, that agreeing with whomever is last in your office, is the politician's stock-in-trade? Put not your trust in princes: consider only their public performances, and not their private promises. One would think that libertarians, at least, would be sensitive to this truth.

And now the whole farce is being repeated once more; again, self-styled libertarians are high up in the Nixon campaign and again they proclaim his devotion to liberty, privately and down deep. Men who have loudly trumpeted their refusal to work with anyone who deviates one iota from the pure libertarian cause are now gleefully paid advisers to Nixon; the deadly smell of power is doing its work. It is almost a good enough reason to take sides in this repellent campaign: to thwart the corrupted ambitions of "libertarians" who have surrendered to the siren song of power.

CHAPTER 56

The New Anarchy

For several years some of us have been proclaiming, unheeded, that the New Left was very different from the Old; that this was not just another embodiment of the old Liberal-Socialist-Communist attitudes and coalition. Now the press is beginning to catch on; everyone knows that the fiery leader of the French student revolution, Daniel (Danny the Red) Cohn-Bendit, is an anarchist and not a socialist, that Red Rudi Dutschke, the German student leader, has at least anarchist tendencies, and that anarchist views permeate the New Left in the United States. C.L. Sulzberger, of the *New York Times*, writes that "the new generation seems nostalgically to be groping toward old-fashioned anarchism." And now even J. Edgar Hoover concedes that the New Left is anarchist rather than communist.

Curiously enough, the attitude of Hoover and other observers seems to hold that anarchists are at least as evil as communists. After a quarter-century of being bombarded with propaganda about the menace of Communism, which we were taught to hate because it was tyrannical statism, we are now supposed to turn around and regard anarchism as perhaps an even *greater* danger because it is totally *against* the state! There is surely something very peculiar going on here. How are we expected to shift our hatreds from arch-statism to ultra-anti-statism so rapidly? And yet, presumably, the public is prepared to do this, so ready are they to shift their hatreds on cue (e.g., from Germany to Russia, from Japan to China) from their rulers.

The answer to this inconsistency is quite evidently that the U.S. government and its Establishment propaganda machine are not in the least bit anti-statist. Their gripe against Communism is *not* that it is statist, but that the Communist Party takes over exclusive control of the state, without making any provisions for cutting in our ruling classes for a piece of the loot. It is this exclusion of the American imperial rulers from shares in the plunder of Communist countries that has set them implacably against Communism. American imperial foreign policy has always been the "Open Door" — an open share in the looting of undeveloped countries. Anti-Communism is a function of the firm Communist closing of that imperial door.

And so, while there are still very few anarchists in the world, the ideological enmity of the American ruling classes toward anarchism is far greater than toward Communism. For anarchism would get rid of the state — all states — completely. It is instructive, by the way, that American imperialism gets along well with those Communist countries which have more or less abandoned the revolutionary, anti-statist side of Communism: Soviet Russia being the outstanding example.

CHAPTER 57

Nixon-Agnew

When they finished nominating Dick Nixon at Miami Beach, the Republican delegates were far from happy at a job well done; instead, they were gloomy, glum, and dispirited. And why not? They had just nominated a two-time loser, a man who had not won any election for eighteen years, a man who inspires no enthusiasm anywhere in the country, a man consistently behind Nelson Rockefeller in the public opinion polls.

That was bad enough. But at least the delegates expected a fresh, appealing, popular face to pep up the ticket, to nail down victory in a very difficult campaign. What they got was a contempt-filled slap in the face. For they found in blank amazement that they were expected to nominate a man whom almost nobody, outside the state of Maryland, had ever heard of: Spiro T. Agnew. Aside from a few of the more honest delegations, the conventioneers swallowed their pride and expressed their loyalty to the ticket; but they left that convention in moods ranging from numb despair to bitter hatred. They had desperately wanted and expected to get a vote-getter to hype the ticket; what they got was one of the most catastrophic bombs in American political history: a man who could attract no votes, but lose many because of the very cynicism of the entire operation.

Why was Agnew picked? Three reasons: What was wanted was a man who was familiar with the cities. Agnew is, but he is not popular with those few who know him, since he takes a tough "shoot-the-looters" line, a line which instead makes him popular in the rural South. Second, he could not be vetoed by any section of the country, surely, since few had ever heard of him. Three, he agrees with Nixon's conservative views on Vietnam and looters, while being so colorless that he couldn't possibly outshine the not very colorful head of the ticket. Nixon, in short, wanted someone to run with him who was a safe, colorless cipher, to go along with a bland campaign which will rest on puerile obeisances to the flag, to motherhood, and to opposition to crime (as if anyone *favors* crime!). Nixon got that cipher in Spiro T. Agnew.

Nixon got his cipher, but in doing so Tricky Dick has outsmarted himself. He has offended not only the Republican Party, but the American people, in picking a choice so far removed from popular will or enthusiasm. Dick Nixon, like Tom Dewey twenty years ago, has managed to snatch defeat from the jaws of victory. Losing seemed a difficult thing for the Republicans this year, but the G.O.P. has once again managed this feat. Unless Hubert Humphrey manages to alienate the American public even more, Richard Nixon has had it; come November he will be a three-time loser, and it couldn't happen to a more deserving fellow, or to a more deserving party.

CHAPTER 58

Speaking Truth To Power

In all the stupefying tedium, hypocrisy, and flatulence of the Republican National Convention, there was only one refreshing moment of truth and candor: when the convention's youngest delegate got up to speak. Paul W. Walter, Jr., twenty-one years old, had unexpectedly won his primary in Cleveland on an anti-Vietnam platform. Now he arose to second the clearly futile, sad, but somehow noble candidacy of Harold E. Stassen for president. To a bored and unheeding audience, Paul Walter addressed these words:

> The 13th Amendment to the United State Constitution specifically prohibits involuntary servitude, and the government is supposed to be the servant of the people. And yet young men who cannot even vote are drafted to kill and to die in a war that is never explained.
>
> We are taught, Thou shalt not kill, do unto others as you would have others do unto you, and love thy neighbor. And yet 10 percent of our Gross National Product is spent on war every year. ... And those few who do not put principle above personal ambition are threatened with prison, such as Dr. Spock, the 20th century Sir Thomas More. Or ridiculed as Governor Stassen, the modern Don Quixote. ...

> These men have helped build the foundation for a lasting peace. The next time we deride them, we should ask if we have done as much . ....
>
> Thank you for your inattention.

The reporter noted, as a supposedly classical symbol of the "generation gap," that Paul Walter, Sr., had been a floor manager for Senator Robert Taft at the 1952 Republican convention. But the reporter was only following cliches and labels, and had forgotten even his recent history. For Senator Taft would have well understood and, I believe, warmly approved, as a veteran battler himself against war and militarism.

In one sense, though, the reporter was quite right. For few people over twenty-one today have been able to grasp what young Walter and the rest of his generation are talking about. For young Walter was, in a real sense, the spokesman for his generation at that convention, and we ignore him only at our peril.

CHAPTER 59

Mao As Free Enterpriser; Or, Halbrook In Wonderland

Mr. [Stephen P.] Halbrook's article in the May *Outlook* is a veritable curiosity, akin to the talking dog or the two-headed man. If nothing else, Mr. Halbrook's portrait of Mao Tse-tung as libertarian and free enterpriser is certainly original. The tone of his thesis, however, has an all-too-familiar quality; one is reminded of nothing so much as the most starry-eyed of the Stalinist tracts of the 1930s: when we were treated to a picture of the happy and productive Soviet society. Under the watchful and benign eye of Comrade Stalin, the happy peasants and the industrious workers busily went about their tasks of Building Socialism and Creating the New Socialist Man, as balalaikas strummed in the background. Comrade Stalin is of course now decidedly unfashionable, and even Mr. Halbrook joins in his denunciation; oddly enough, one of the very few people who still quote Stalin with reverence is none other than Comrade Mao, whom Halbrook would offer to us as the great anti-Stalinist of our epoch. But the same *leitmotif* is there; note, for example, how the defects and evils which Mr. Halbrook sometimes concedes to exist in Communist China are *always* and unfailingly attributed to bad guys who worked against or betrayed the great Chairman, in the same way, in the 1930s, whatever flaws were conceded to be in Soviet society were invariably due to bad guys (Trotsky, Bukharin, et al.) who had betrayed the Stalinist vision. Eventually, one begins to wonder how a Leader of such

---

Reprinted from *Outlook*, July 8, 1972.

greatness and infallibility could always surround himself with hand-picked comrades who invariably betray him and his policies.

As for Halbrook's curious portrayal of Mao and the Cultural Revolution as free-marketeers it is enough to point to Professor Walter Galenson's recent review of the Maoist tract by Wheelwright and McFarlane,[1] on which Halbrook relies for much of his thesis. Galenson points out what every student of China knows: that these Maoist authors portray the goals of Maoism as: universal dedication by every individual to "serve the people"; the abolition of material incentives "and their replacement by moral and ideological drives"; "the rejection of profit as a criterion of efficiency"; and, last, but not least, "the rejection of mass consumption as a social goal." Wheelwright and McFarlane join Mao in condemning Liu Shao-chi for the crime of "raising output and productivity by the non-Maoist expedients of 'putting profits in command,' of emphasizing expertness rather than 'redness' as qualification for managerial jobs, of differentiating pay, and of using the market to distribute goods."

But enough: there is no need for a libertarian to engage in a sober and quiet refutation of the thesis that the creator of the most totalitarian nation in the history of mankind has really been leading his people into a libertarian and even — ye gods! — a "free-market" Utopia. I am reminded of an instructive incident of a few years ago, when a young Maoist of my acquaintance took a flight out of Hanoi on a Communist Chinese airline. It was a flight in which "bourgeois individualism" was sweetly but firmly transcended. As the loudspeaker played incessantly the Red Chinese anthem, "East is Red," the stewardess went up to the young American, pressed a song book into his hand, and quietly but firmly insisted that he sing along; refusal to sing would, of course, be taken as an indication of hostility to the "mass line" and to the Chinese people. It was a short flight; but when he emerged, shaken and sweating a bit, the bloom of the Maoist Utopia had faded for good. One begins to think that it is far, far easier to idolize Chairman Mao amidst the comfort of a Florida campus than it would be in Peking or, worse yet, in some agricultural commune in Sinkiang.

It is far more interesting to ponder the question: how did Stephen Halbrook get this way? How in the world could he begin as a full-fledged and ardent libertarian, and then rapidly proceed to the point of being a worshipful and adoring Maoist overlaid with a patina of libertarian rhetoric?

---

[1]Walter Galenson, "Review of E.L. Wheelwright and Bruce McFarlane, *The Chinese Road to Socialism*," *Journal of Economic Literature* (March, 1972), p. 80.

Halbrook is correct in the point that Liu Shao-chi was a bureaucrat and centralist, and that Mao's "Cultural Revolution" was indeed a prodding of the masses to destroy the Communist Party and the (then existing) State apparatus. Even here, however, his implication that the State *per se* has been smashed in China is grotesque: what happened was that the Army took over the state functions. Furthermore, Halbrook fails to mention the fact that his heroes on the "left wing" of the Cultural Revolution, notably Lin Piao, have now been repudiated and purged by Mao, and that a functioning State apparatus has been reconstituted under Chou En-lai. But let us omit this and concentrate on the aims of the "left" Cultural Revolutionaries. Yes, they were against central planning; yes, they were opposed to bureaucracy; but does this make them libertarians and free-marketeers?

The problem is that Halbrook has been misled by the anti-centralizing and anti-bureaucratic rhetoric and policies. He could indeed have strengthened his case for the moment by pointing out that Mao, in his early days, was an avowed Anarchist before he became a Marxist. But the nub of the problem is that the "anarchism," the anti-centralism toward which the Cultural Revolutionaries were pointing, was *not* individualist anarchism, or free-market capitalism. It was, rather, left-wing anarchism, or "anarcho-communism." The drive to establish decentralized communes, the push toward self-sufficiency of these communes, all of these were attempts to arrive at the anarcho-communist goal by coercive, statist means. The lesson that this should drive home to every libertarian is that we have nothing in common with communist anarchists; that their goals would mean death for the individual, death for his happiness and productivity, and death, too, for the human race, as a result of the stamping out of the division of labor which is the goal of every true communist, be he anarchist or not.

At the heart of the matter is Halbrook's adulation of the Great Leap Forward of the late 1950s. For the Great Leap was a desperate attempt by Mao — one of the last of the "fundamentalist" communists on the world scene — to leap into communism at one blow. The Soviets, for all their bureaucracy and statism, did have the great good sense to abandon long ago the communist dream, and to push it off to a remote future, after productivity shall have been enormously increased. But the Maoists, heedless of economics, heedless of the terribly destructive effects on production of abolishing the division of labor — the essence of the "communist stage" — tried to hurl themselves into Utopia. Halbrook is surely one of the few people in the world who think of the Great Leap Forward as a success; even the Chinese Communists themselves were reluctantly forced to abandon that Leap, because of the economic collapse that came about through the attempts, for example, to build steel plants in every backyard. Just as Lenin prudently retreated from "War Communism" when he saw the economic disaster it had brought, so did Mao retreat from the Great Leap Forward when *its* disaster became starkly evident to everyone but Steve Halbrook. The Cultural Revolution was another attempt to accomplish a similar goal; and it too has been abandoned.

But the costs of these attempts — in human and in economic terms — were enormous. In each try the key was the attempt to abolish the division of labor; to eliminate what the Marxists idiotically call the "contradiction between intellectual and physical labor" and the "contradiction between industry and countryside." (For "contradiction," read specialization and the division of labor.) That is why every rural commune had to have its own steel plant; and that is why, during the Cultural Revolution, all the schools were closed for several years, and millions of students shipped permanently to rural frontiers such as Sinkiang so as to "eliminate their contradiction between intellectual and physical labor." And this is what *all* types of communism, whether "anarchist" or Maoist, mean in the end: an evil, ant heap society of faceless automatons, with all individuality, and all individual development, stamped out by the fanatical ideologues of egalitarianism.

To say that the herding of millions of students, for example, into frontier communes was "voluntary" is surely a grotesque perversion of the term. But there is something more at stake here, for the centralizing State is not the *only* enemy of individual liberty; for the communist ideal (anarchist or Maoist) involves a *total* tyranny over each person by his own beloved decentralized commune. And that is why it is China, not Russia, which has mobilized every block, every acre of earth, into local committees in which the soul of every individual member is laid bare and tyrannized over by his neighbors. Every member is forced or induced to confess his sins in public "self-criticism" sessions: the sins, of course, being any deviation from the opinion of his "decentralized" neighbors. And the "material" incentives to production are to be stamped out in favor of an egalitarian "moral" incentive in which the "good of the mass" is supposedly the individual's only incentive for work and action.

No sir; if I were forced to choose between the Russian and the Chinese societies, I would take the Russian every time. For all its bureaucracy and statism, Russia does have a developed division of labor and at least the rudiments of a market, and hence a fairly productive economy; and, in abandoning its absurd goal of communism, the Russian society provides at least a portion of room for individuality and for personal freedom. For the libertarian, the triumph of Mao over Liu was something to deplore and not to cheer about; the main hope for the future of China, indeed, is that Mao and his fanatical comrades are all aging rapidly; that the younger generation cannot, after all, be imbued with the same revolutionary fervor; and that therefore the adoption of the Russian — and perhaps eventually the infinitely freer Yugoslavian — modes is the most likely prognosis for the Chinese future.

But again: how did Steve Halbrook get that way? The devolution of Mr. Halbrook is an object lesson for all libertarians, a lesson in the destructive pursuit of a one-sided logic. A few years ago, several militant libertarians began the instructive process of needling the right wing, of correcting the errors of a simplistic anti-Communism that had diverted the Right from opposition to the State itself. Pursuing this corrective beyond sensible bounds, Mr. Halbrook has lamentably wound up as an apologist for rampant totalitarianism.

CHAPTER 60

Defusing the Baby Bomb

One of the longer lasting aspects of the Great Ecology Scare of the 1969–70 intellectual season (a craze which seems to have faded away since the orgiastic exercises of "Earth Day"), is the Population Hysteria. The Left has clasped to its collective bosom the idea that population growth is the root cause of our Environmental Crisis, and Zero Population Growth clubs have sprouted over the nation's colleges. Young men and women solemnly take the pledge never to have more than two children and thereby cause population growth. What is far worse, the same people are just as convinced that no one *be allowed* to have more than her two-child quota. Hardly have we begun to be freed from the tyranny of the *outlawry* of birth control, when, lo and behold!, birth control is now to be made *compulsory*.[1]

---

[1]Particularly grotesque is the "free-market" variant of this slave measure proposed by the distinguished economist Kenneth Boulding. Boulding would maximize individual freedom within the Zero Population Growth framework by granting every woman (or is it wife?) two baby-rights, and then permit women to sell these baby-rights to one another. So that if one woman wished to have four kids she could do so, but only if two other women limited their number to one apiece, or one decided to go without. Which makes about as much "free market" sense as allowing a market in slaves.

Reprinted from *The Individualist*, January 1971.

There is no need to detail here the monstrous tyranny entailed by this fascistic proposal. We need only remark that it is curious that the same leftists who properly assert every woman's absolute right over her own body in denouncing abortion laws, are grossly inconsistent in not applying this very right to every woman's right to bear children. Hopefully, Justice [Arthur] Goldberg's remarkable landmark decision in the Connecticut birth-control case, striking down that law for invasion of the Ninth Amendment natural right of privacy, will suffice to block any compulsory birth control law.[2] Even at that time, the anti-populationists, while hailing the decision, grumbled that the bringing in of the Ninth Amendment might destroy their cherished goal of compulsory birth control.[3]

Apart from the question of compulsion, what of the Population Problem? Are we suffering from "too much" population? The first question to ask is simply: how much is "too much?" Why has it suddenly become imperative to freeze the U.S. population at its present level of approximately 200 million? Also, why stop at 200 million? Is this a divinely imposed figure? Why not press on to allowing only one kid per family, thereby soon cutting the population in half? Or allow only one kid per ten families? Or, indeed, go the whole way by arbitrarily killing every tenth, or every fifth, or whatever person?

In short, how much is too much? Before the European colonization, the North American continent supported less than one million Indians, and these at near-starvation levels. That continent now supports almost three hundred million people, at enormously greater and, what is more, growing affluence. It should be clear, then, that the "proper" population level must be relative to the capital equipment and the industrial development of the area. A land area that barely supported

---

[2]*Griswold v. Connecticut* (1965). Before this case, the Supreme Court, recognizing the enormous libertarian implications of the Ninth Amendment, had never dared to apply it. The Ninth Amendment reads: "The enumeration in the Constitution of certain rights, shall not be construed to deny or disparage others retained by the people." Thus, the Amendment flatly states that the people do retain other rights, and what are they? Anyone understanding the terminology of the time knows that this means natural rights, and among such is the now-proclaimed right to privacy. On the Ninth Amendment and its significance see Bennett B. Patterson, *The Forgotten Ninth Amendment* (Indianapolis: Bobbs-Merrill, 1955); "Discovering the Ninth Amendment," *Left and Right* (Autumn, 1965), pp. 8–12.

[3]See James D. Carroll, "The Forgotten Amendment," *The Nation* (September 6, 1965), pp. 8–12,

one million people five hundred years ago now very readily supports three hundred times that number.

The question: how much is too much, then, can only be answered in the context of the capital and the extent of the market enjoyed by the economic system. The only cogent criterion, which has been worked out by economists, and which is never mentioned by the Population Hysterics, is the concept of the "optimum population" point. Setting aside the unfortunate moralistic connotation of the term, that this is the morally proper or best population level, the optimum population concept focuses on the point that, given any particular level of capital and technology, as we increase the population hypothetically from zero, the economy's total production per head will increase, will eventually level off, and finally decline. That population level which, for any given capital and technology, yields the maximum production per person — the highest standard of living per person — is the "optimum" level.

Take, for example, the present United States economy. Suppose that a natural disaster suddenly wipes out three-fourths of the U.S. population. It is obvious that total production per head will fall drastically, simply because an enormous amount of equipment and jobs will lie idle for lack of workers. On the other hand, if the population of the U.S. should magically triple tonight, obviously the total production per head would also fall, since the given equipment would hardly absorb, or suffice, for the additional labor force. Somewhere in between lies the optimum population point.

Empirically, it is impossible to say for certain where this population point lies, whether we are at present below or above it. But one thing is certain: the production per person has continued to increase steadily in the United States, despite all the shackling of the market economy and despite (or helped by?) the continuing population growth. As long as the standard of living continues to rise, we surely cannot be very much beyond the optimum population level, if at all, and we surely have little or nothing to worry about on the score of population. Furthermore, while the economy grows, while capital increases and technology improves, as they have continued to do, the optimum population level continues to increase, just as it has already increased from far below a million to about two hundred million. The Population Scare is just that: still another bogey designed to scare the American public into more statist dictation.

Furthermore, the rate of population growth is not simply an arbitrary given; it has always been highly responsive to social and economic conditions. Before the advent of capitalism and the Industrial Revolution, population was indeed an enormous problem; for population in the famous words of Malthus, kept "pressing on the means of subsistence." Population growth is the spectre that haunts all frozen, caste, pre-industrial societies; for a caste system can assign the son of a carpenter to be a carpenter as well, but what is to be done with the second son? It was the specter of population growth, and not some sort of unusually barbaric streak in their character, that caused the Spartans to put their newborn babies out into the woods overnight; it was their form of "population control."

But all this was changed with modern capitalism and the Industrial Revolution. For now a rapidly growing and developing economy at last replaced the frozen systems of status. The enormous growth of capital and production enabled a great growth of population, largely by slashing the death rate. But, as in every subsequent case of a growing standard of living, this cut in the death rate was soon followed by a cut in the birth rate by people who wanted to preserve their new-found improvement in living conditions. It is precisely the undeveloped nations of Asia, for example, who have not enjoyed the benefits of capitalist development, whose birth rate remains high, and who may be said to suffer from "overpopulation." But, the United States and Europe, who have enjoyed rising living standards, have far lower birth rates; in short, people attune themselves to higher living standards, and then make sure they are preserved by voluntarily lowering their birth rates.

Again, then "over-population" is not an absolute, but strictly relative to the capital and technology of the land areas concerned. India is now "over-populated" for much the same reason that the United States would also be overpopulated if we only had the capital equipment and the market development of a century ago to service our two hundred million population. All this is well illustrated by the case of Japan. Eager to develop and industrialize rapidly after World War II, Japan encouraged birth control among its public to cut down on its seeming "over-population." Now, however, with the same meager land area and virtual absence of natural resources but with a flourishing industrial economy and a very rapid growth rate, Japan finds, on the contrary, that it is beginning to suffer from a labor shortage — that it cannot fill the jobs available. As a result, it is wisely beginning to drop its artificial encouragements to birth control.

That "over" or "under" population are strictly relative to time and place is also seen by the fact that by no means all underdeveloped areas are in any sense densely populated. Just as the Indians of North America were only "overpopulated" in relation to their capital and technology, so are most areas of Africa and South America — in contrast to Asia — quite sparsely populated, especially in relation to their natural resources. What they lack is capital — and capitalism; given that, they would require a far greater population than they have today.

As for the United States, its birth rate has, over the long run and in recent years, tended downward. In fact, during the 1930s the birth rate was so low in the United States and particularly in France, that cries arose of imminent "racial suicide." What happened was that after World War II, the desire for roots among returning GI's, along with a sudden upsurge (now gone) in pro-baby values in our culture, led to the famous "baby boom," and to a consequent acceleration of population growth. But that baby boom is now over, and the U.S. birth rate began tending downwards in 1957. The rate of U.S. population growth in the decade of the sixties was only 14%, the second lowest decennial increase on record. By 1969, in fact, the average increase of the U.S. population was only 1 percent per year, less than half the world rate, and the American birth rate was the lowest ever recorded in this country.[4] The United States, furthermore, remains lower in population density (average number of persons per square mile), than such relatively uncrowded countries as Britain, Mexico, or Switzerland.

Not only that, but within the United States, far from population growth filling all the open spaces, there is actually, as Professor Wrong points out, "more open space in the United States today then there was a generation ago, and ... much of it is actual or potential farmland in the middle of the country."[5] In the decade of the sixties fully one-third of all the counties in the U.S. actually lost population (Zero Population Growth fulfilled with a vengeance!), most of them in the South and Middle West. In fact, since 1966, the central cities of the United States have been steadily losing population as well.

Under steadily growing capitalism, then, the Population Scare is a bogey from two directions: the optimum population point tends to

[4]See Dennis H. Wrong, "Portrait of a Decade," *New York Sunday Times Magazine* (August 2, 1970), pp. 22ff.

[5]Ibid., p. 27.

increase continually; and the birth rate tends to level off naturally to preserve the higher living standards.

We have seen that the population problem is strictly relative to the economic conditions of a time and place; one country's or one era's "over-population" can easily become the opposite, and vice versa if economic growth is shackled or reversed. In fact, the Population Hysterics are, presumably unwittingly, trying desperately to create the very problem they are bellyaching about. For we have seen that population growth is no problem under growing and developing capitalism. But it does become a real problem when the economy is prevented from growing, when the progress under capitalism is replaced by frozen status. And since the anti-populationists are also opposed to economic growth in order to "save" scarce natural resources, this means that the Environmentalists, if they are allowed their way, will create the over-population menace which so far has been only a phantasm of their own making. Allow these opponents of progress their head, and we too can become another Sparta.

If the population question is relative to capital and technology, it is also relative to something else that is very important but that "nice" people don't like to talk about: the quality of the population. In short, it we deal only with quantities, with the numbers of people in different age groups, etc., we are in danger of forgetting that one person is not equivalent to another. A country or a region can be "over-populated" if the citizenry are lacking the qualities of hard work, thrift, and entrepreneurial foresight; let people enter the country with these very qualities, and both they and the original citizens will benefit. Even given existing capital, then, the country would not be "over-populated" with respect to these more productive and more entrepreneurial groups. In fact, few countries at few times are anything but short of such highly productive citizens.

To illustrate the importance of population quality, consider the Chinese — in general a highly productive and entrepreneurial group. They have migrated to other "over-populated" parts of Asia, coming, it should be noted, with little or no capital, and just as poor — if not more so — than the indigenous population. And yet, within a few years, these Chinese will have risen, become wealthy, created jobs and prosperity for themselves and much of the native population. The same is true of Lebanese who migrated to the "overpopulated" West Indies.[6]

---

[6]Thus, the leading economist of "underdeveloped" countries writes:

While we have used the concept of optimum population to explode the Population Bomb, we must recognize that even this concept makes too many concessions to the anti-populationists. First, because of its neglect of the differences in population quality; and second, because of the implicit assumption that the "optimum" is the morally correct. But people obviously have children because they want to and enjoy having them, and therefore people may well decide to accept a lower than optimum production per man in order to benefit from the enjoyment of having more children. A family might have four children instead of two, even though it knows that it will have a lower standard of living per member of the family. And surely that decision, that choice between the competing benefits of having more or less children, at lower or higher standards of living, is strictly up to each person, to each family to make. Their own free choice is the moral "optimum," and not the imposed ethical standard of some outside observer.

There is something else of importance that we may say about the anti-populationists. It may seem extreme to say this, but they are not simply anti-population, they are also anti-people. Libertarians and opponents of the welfare state are accustomed to being denounced as "inhumane"; but it is the Environmentalists who are profoundly and deeply anti-human. Consider their basic social philosophy. Before the advent of man, they assert, everything was marvelous. Nature was in perfect harmony with itself, and each species of life lived in harmonious ecological balance with each other. They had to, since each species was passively determined by

"The Chinese in Malaya, the Indians in East Africa, and Lebanese in West Africa — usually migrants without capital and without much formal education — have quite soon greatly surpassed the economic performance of the indigenous population. ... These differences in economic quality and performance are also relevant to overpopulation and population pressure. There is heavy emigration from the West Indies, which are said to be severely overpopulated. Yet the Lebanese are anxious to migrate to the West Indies, and those few who are admitted generally prosper and accumulate capital. Thus even at current levels of technique the West Indies are not overpopulated in terms of Lebanese although they are in terms of West Indians." Peter T. Bauer, *Economic Analysis and Policy in Underdeveloped Countries* (Durham, N.C.: Duke University Press, 1957), pp. 74–76. On the crippling effects of immigration restrictions on Lebanese in West Africa, see P.T. Bauer and B.S. Yamey, "Economic Aspects of Immigration Policy in Nigeria and the Gold Coast," *South African Journal of Economics* (1954), 223–232.

its given environment, by the "nature" in which it found himself. Then, in the midst of this perfect harmonious idyll, there came the great disturber, the great pain-in-the-neck: man. Man, by his nature, is not passively determined by his environment; and so man began to survive and flourish by transforming his environment, by changing things, by "conquering nature" instead of being determined by its "rhythms." While the rest of nature is determined and "circular," man persists in being purposeful and "linear," endlessly changing his environment to improve his lot. The basic aim of the Environmentalists is to eradicate this purposefulness of man, to shackle his linearity and purpose, to reduce him to the primitive, animal status of a species "in harmony with nature" instead of its master. But this means, in essence, that the Environmentalists are bent upon eradicating man's humanity, and therefore on destroying the human race itself. Jack Bulloff, professor of the history of science at SUNY, Albany, does not exaggerate when he writes:

> The first idea [of the Environmentalists] holds that the natural environment is benign. To leave it alone, or restore it, would solve all environmental problems. But the record of two billion years is directly contrary to this. Paleontology is a record of the dead. ... Nature is inevitably lethal. ...
>
> Certainly man pollutes. But he cannot survive otherwise. Man saved himself and advanced from animal to civilized being only by overcoming the lethal natural environment. By imposing social evolution on biological evolution man created an environment far more suited to human life than the mythical bliss of pre-social man. ...
>
> It is strange that [the Environmentalists] ... should hunger for the unsafe, unenlightened, unaesthetic life of the savage. The idea that a world safe for rhinoceroses — or cobras or doddoes — is best for man appeals only in its innocences. Its proponents are really advocating genocide.[7]

Is there nothing we can do, then, about the Population Problem? Are there no measures that we can advocate? On the contrary, there are several

---

[7]Jack Bulloff, "A World Safe for Rhinos Is Not Best for Men," *University Review* (State University of New York), Summer 1970.

things we can do, none of which, oddly enough, I have ever seen propounded by our Population Hysterics. We can return to (or rather, advance toward) laissez-faire by removing the host of government subsidies to population growth. We can remove the myriad governmental incentives for having more children. For example, we can stop levying higher income taxes on bachelors or on childless couples than on couples with children. The income tax system now subsidizes large families by levying taxes in inverse proportion to the number of children. We can also end the policy of the welfare system in paying welfare mothers per child, once again subsidizing larger and larger families, this time among mothers who can least afford to raise them. And finally, we can end the free public school system, which taxes bachelors and childless couples for the benefit of families with children and the more numerous the children the greater the subsidy. When families will have to pay for their own education, then this artificial and coerced subsidy to large families will be removed. Let us think in terms of achieving freedom by removing subsidies to larger families, rather than agitate to impose a coercive despotism on us all in behalf of a Population Myth that reflects a deep-seated hostility to the human race itself.

CHAPTER 61

The New Libertarian Creed

Recently a great deal of publicity has been given to a burgeoning split in the right wing, a split between the dominant Buckley-*National Review* conservatives and the new libertarians.

In their breakaway, the libertarians, who are strong on college campuses and generally among the youth, hark back to an older, almost forgotten tradition of individualism that characterized the right wing in the 1930s and 40s. Led by such notable intellectuals as Albert Jay Nock and H.L. Mencken, and by the Taft wing of the Republican party among the politicians, the older right wing was devoted to the liberty of the individual.

It therefore led the opposition to the growth of Big Government in America, a growth presided over by New Deal–Fair Deal liberalism. This older right wing upheld civil liberty and the economic freedom of the market economy while opposing government intervention, conscription, militarism and American intervention and imperialism overseas.

Since the mid-1950s, however, the *National Review* has led the right into its present conservative stance. In rhetoric, the *National Review* upholds a "fusion" of liberty and order: in which the liberty of the individual is judiciously contained within a matrix of order supplied by the state. In his early days, William Buckley proclaimed himself a libertarian, with the single exception of the need to wage an all-out struggle against the

Reprinted from the *New York Times*, February 9, 1971.

"Communist conspiracy," at home and abroad. This concession was bad enough, as the entire thrust of conservative foreign policy was redirected toward militarism and empire.

But since the mid-50s, as the conservative movement has moved ever closer to the seats of power, whatever libertarian elements had been in the "fusion" have one by one disappeared. And so the *National Review* now supports, with scarcely a qualm, the gigantic misinvestment of the SST [supersonic transport] and space programs, the nationalization of passenger rail service, restrictions on imports, and virtually the entire Nixon program. It warmly supports laws enforcing moral codes, and opposes civil liberties, as well as the American tradition of separation of church and state. It was in response to this systematic shedding of their libertarian strands that so many right-wing youth have rebelled and have taken out on their own. The tensions of the attempt to fuse liberty and order have finally split the conservative coalition apart.

The libertarian doctrine begins, not with the conservative community or state but with the individual. Every individual as an independent acting entity possesses the absolute right of "self-ownership"; that is, to own his or her person without molestation by others. From this axiom we derive total opposition to conscription and abortion laws. Secondly, each individual then has the right to own any previously unowned resources (such as virgin land) that he finds and brings into use by exerting his personal energy upon the resource. From this is derived the right of "homesteading" landed property, and, as a consequence, all the other rights of private property. For if a man owns himself and his homesteaded land, he also has the right to own unmolested the land that he has transformed into capital, as well as the right to give his property to anyone he wishes (hence the right of inheritance) and to exchange his titles to property for anyone else's titles (hence the right of free contract and the *laissez-faire* free-market economy).

The conservative holds as one of his highest goals the preservation of "law and order," but his "order" and his "law" is the coercive dictation of the state. Throughout the ages, and in the present day as well, the state has lived through the profound disorder of continuing aggression against the person and property of countless individuals. It robs through taxation, enslaves through conscription and murders by way of club, bayonet, napalm and H-bombs. The libertarian holds that the state is permanent aggression and disorder, and that the *National Review* conservatives constitute some of the state's most articulate champions and apologists.

The young libertarians are not simply returning to Taft-era individualism. In asserting themselves as libertarians they are returning as well to the tradition which once established America as the proud beacon-light of freedom, the tradition of Jefferson, Paine, Jackson and Garrison. And in doing so, they are repudiating such conservative theorists as James Burnham, editor of the *National Review*, who has conceded that there is no rational foundation for government, and has asserted, in a reversion to the ancient despotic theories of divine right, that "in ancient times, before the illusions of science had corrupted traditional wisdom, the founders of cities (states) were known to be gods or demigods."

Burnham's recent call in *National Review* for a new Bismarck for America and for a re-evaluation of fascism is the logical culmination of conservative statism and obscurantism. The libertarians, in contrast, are raising the standards of freedom and reason on which this country was founded.

CHAPTER 62

Confessions of a Right-Wing Liberal

Twenty years ago I was an extreme right-wing Republican, a young and lone "Neanderthal" (as the liberals used to call us) who believed, as one friend pungently put it, that "Senator Taft had sold out to the socialists." Today, I am most likely to be called an extreme leftist, since I favor immediate withdrawal from Vietnam, denounce US imperialism, advocate Black Power and have just joined the new Peace and Freedom Party. And yet my basic political views have not changed by a single iota in these two decades!

It is obvious that something is very wrong with the old labels, with the categories of "left" and "right," and with the ways in which we customarily apply these categories to American political life. My personal odyssey is unimportant; the important point is that if I can move from "extreme right" to "extreme left" merely by standing in one place, drastic though unrecognized changes must have taken place throughout the American political spectrum over the last generation.

I joined the right-wing movement — to give a formal name to a very loose and informal set of associations — as a young graduate student shortly after the end of World War II. There was no question as to where the intellectual right of that day stood on militarism and conscription: it opposed them as instruments of mass slavery and mass murder. Conscription, indeed, was thought far worse than other forms of statist controls

Reprinted from *Ramparts*, June 15, 1968.

and incursions, for while these only appropriated part of the individual's property, the draft, like slavery, took his most precious possession: his own person. Day after day the veteran publicist John T. Flynn — once praised as a liberal and then condemned as a reactionary, with little or no change in his views — inveighed implacably in print and over the radio against militarism and the draft. Even the Wall Street newspaper, the *Commercial and Financial Chronicle*, published a lengthy attack on the idea of conscription.

All of our political positions, from the free market in economics to opposing war and militarism, stemmed from our root belief in individual liberty and our opposition to the state. Simplistically, we adopted the standard view of the political spectrum: "left" meant socialism, or total power of the state; the further "right" one went the less government one favored. Hence, we called ourselves "extreme rightists."

Originally, our historical heroes were such men as Jefferson, Paine, [Richard] Cobden, [John] Bright and [Herbert] Spencer; but as our views became purer and more consistent, we eagerly embraced such near-anarchists as the voluntarist, Auberon Herbert, and the American individualist-anarchists, Lysander Spooner and Benjamin R. Tucker. One of our great intellectual heroes was Henry David Thoreau, and his essay, "Civil Disobedience," was one of our guiding stars. Right-wing theorist Frank Chodorov devoted an entire issue of his monthly, *Analysis*, to an appreciation of Thoreau.

In our relation to the remainder of the American political scene, we of course recognized that the extreme right of the Republican Party was not made up of individualist anti-statists, but they were close enough to our position to make us feel part of a quasi-libertarian united front. Enough of our views were present among the extreme members of the Taft wing of the Republican Party (much more so than in Taft himself, who was among the most liberal of that wing), and in such organs as the *Chicago Tribune*, to make us feel quite comfortable with this kind of alliance.

What is more, the right-wing Republicans were major opponents of the Cold War. Valiantly, the extreme rightist Republicans, who were particularly strong in the House, battled conscription, NATO and the Truman Doctrine. Consider, for example, Omaha's Representative Howard Buffett, Senator Taft's midwestern campaign manager in 1952. He was one of the most extreme of the extremists, once described by *The Nation* as "an able young man whose ideas have tragically fossilized."

I came to know Buffett as a genuine and thoughtful libertarian. Attacking the Truman Doctrine on the floor of Congress, he declared: "Even if it were desirable, America is not strong enough to police the world by military force. If that attempt is made, the blessings of liberty will be replaced by coercion and tyranny at home. Our Christian ideals cannot be exported to other lands by dollars and guns."

When the Korean War came, almost the entire old left, with the exception of the Communist Party, surrendered to the global mystique of the United Nations and "collective security against aggression," and backed Truman's imperialist aggression in that war. Even Corliss Lamont backed the American stand in Korea. Only the extreme rightist Republicans continued to battle U.S. imperialism. It was the last great political outburst of the Old Right of my youth.

Howard Buffett was convinced that the United States was largely responsible for the eruption of conflict in Korea; for the rest of his life he tried unsuccessfully to get the Senate Armed Services Committee to declassify the testimony of CIA head Admiral [Roscoe H.] Hillenkoeter, which Buffett told me established American responsibility for the Korean outbreak. The last famous isolationist move came late in December 1950, after the Chinese forces had beaten the Americans out of North Korea. Joseph P. Kennedy and Herbert Hoover delivered two ringing speeches back-to-back calling for American evacuation of Korea. As Hoover put it, "To commit the sparse ground forces of the non-communist nations into a land war against this communist land mass [in Asia] would be a war without victory, a war without a successful political terminal ... that would be the graveyard of millions of American boys" and the exhaustion of the United States. Joe Kennedy declared that "if portions of Europe or Asia wish to go communistic or even have communism thrust upon them, we cannot stop it."

To this *The Nation* replied with typical liberal Red-baiting: "The line they are laying down for their country should set the bells ringing in the Kremlin as nothing has since the triumph of Stalingrad"; and the *New Republic* actually saw Stalin sweeping onwards "until the Stalinist caucus in the Tribune Tower would bring out in triumph the first communist edition of the *Chicago Tribune*."

The main catalyst for transforming the mass base of the right wing from an isolationist and quasi-libertarian movement to an anti-communist one was probably "McCarthyism." Before Senator Joe McCarthy launched his anti-communist crusade in February 1950, he had not been particularly associated with the right wing of the Republican Party; on the contrary, his record was liberal and centrist, statist rather than libertarian.

Furthermore, Red-baiting and anti-communist witch hunting were originally launched by liberals, and even after McCarthy the liberals were the most effective at this game. It was, after all, the liberal Roosevelt Administration which passed the Smith Act, first used against Trotskyites and isolationists during World War II and then against communists after the war; it was the liberal Truman Administration that instituted loyalty checks; it was the eminently liberal Hubert Humphrey who was a sponsor of the clause in the McCarran Act of 1950 threatening concentration camps for "subversives."

McCarthy not only shifted the focus of the right to communist hunting, however. His crusade also brought into the right wing a new mass base. Before McCarthy, the rank-and-file of the right wing was the small-town, isolationist middle west. McCarthyism brought into the movement a mass of urban Catholics from the eastern seaboard, people whose outlook on individual liberty was, if anything, negative.

If McCarthy was the main catalyst for mobilizing the mass base of the new right, the major ideological instrument of the transformation was the blight of anti-communism, and the major carriers were Bill Buckley and *National Review*.

In the early days, young Bill Buckley often liked to refer to himself as an "individualist," sometimes even as an "anarchist." But all these libertarian ideals, he maintained, had to remain in total abeyance, fit only for parlor discussion, until the great crusade against the "international communist conspiracy" had been driven to a successful conclusion. Thus, as early as January 1952, I noted with disquiet an article that Buckley wrote for *Commonweal*, "A Young Republican's View."

He began the article in a splendid libertarian manner: our enemy, he affirmed, was the state, which, he quoted Spencer, was "begotten of aggression and by aggression." But then came the worm in the apple: the anti-communist crusade had to be waged. Buckley went on to endorse "the extensive and productive tax laws that are needed to support a vigorous anti-communist foreign policy"; he declared that the "thus far invincible aggressiveness of the Soviet Union" imminently threatened American security, and that therefore "we have to accept Big Government for the duration — for neither an offensive nor a defensive war can be waged ... except through the instrument of a totalitarian bureaucracy within our shores." Therefore, he concluded — in the midst of the Korean War — we must all support "large armies and air forces, atomic energy, central intelligence, war production boards and the attendant centralization of power in Washington."

The right wing, never articulate, has not had many organs of opinion. Therefore, when Buckley founded *National Review* in late 1955, its erudite, witty and glib editorials and articles swiftly made it the only politically relevant journal for the American right. Immediately, the ideological line of the right began to change sharply.

One element that gave special fervor and expertise to the Red-baiting crusade was the prevalence of ex-communists, ex-fellow travelers and ex-Trotskyites among the writers whom *National Review* brought into prominence on the right-wing scene. These ex-leftists were consumed with an undying hatred for their former love, along with a passion for bestowing enormous importance upon their apparently wasted years. Almost the entire older generation of writers and editors for *National Review* had been prominent in the old left. Some names that come to mind are: Jim Burnham, John Chamberlain, Whittaker Chambers, Ralph de Toledano, Will Herberg, Eugene Lyons, J.B. Matthews, Frank S. Meyer, William S. Schlamm and Karl Wittfogel.

An insight into the state of mind of many of these people came in a recent letter to me from one of the most libertarian of this group; he admitted that my stand in opposition to the draft was the only one consistent with libertarian principles, but, he said, he can't forget how nasty the communist cell in *Time* magazine was in the 1930s. The world is falling apart and yet these people are still mired in the petty grievances of faction fights of long ago!

Anti-communism was the central root of the decay of the old libertarian right, but it was not the only one. In 1953, a big splash was made by the publication of Russell Kirk's *The Conservative Mind.* Before that, no one on the right regarded himself as a "conservative"; "conservative" was considered a left smear word. Now, suddenly, the right began to glory in the term "conservative," and Kirk began to make speaking appearances, often in a kind of friendly "vital center" tandem with Arthur Schlesinger, Jr.

This was to be the beginning of the burgeoning phenomenon of the friendly-though-critical dialogue between the liberal and conservative wings of the Great Patriotic American Consensus. A new, younger generation of rightists, of "conservatives," began to emerge, who thought that the real problem of the modern world was nothing so ideological as the state vs. individual liberty or government intervention vs. the free market; the real problem, they declared, was the preservation of tradition, order,

Christianity and good manners against the modern sins of reason, license, atheism and boorishness.

One of the first dominant thinkers of this new right was Buckley's brother-in-law, L. Brent Bozell, who wrote fiery articles in *National Review* attacking liberty even as an abstract principle (and not just as something to be temporarily sacrificed for the benefit of the anti-communist emergency). The function of the state was to impose and enforce moral and religious principles.

Another repellent political theorist who made his mark in *National Review* was the late Willmoore Kendall, *NR* editor for many years. His great thrust was the right and the duty of the majority of the community — as embodied, say, in Congress — to suppress any individual who disturbs that community with radical doctrines. Socrates, opined Kendall, not only *should* have been killed by the Greek community, whom he offended by his subversive criticisms, but it was their moral *duty* to kill him.

The historical heroes of the new right were changing rapidly. Mencken, Nock, Thoreau, Jefferson, Paine — all these either dropped from sight or were soundly condemned as rationalists, atheists or anarchists. From Europe, the "in" people were now such despotic reactionaries as Burke, Metternich, de Maistre; in the United States, Hamilton and Madison were "in," with their stress on the imposition of order and a strong, elitist central government — which included the southern "slavocracy."

For the first few years of its existence, I moved in *National Review* circles, attended its editorial luncheons, wrote articles and book reviews for the magazine; indeed, there was talk at one time of my joining the staff as an economics columnist.

I became increasingly alarmed, however, as *NR* and its friends grew in strength because I knew, from innumerable conversations with rightist intellectuals, what their foreign policy goal was. They never quite dared to state it publicly, although they would slyly imply it and would try to whip the public up to the fever pitch of demanding it. What they wanted — and still want — was nuclear annihilation of the Soviet Union. They want to drop that Bomb on Moscow. (Of course, on Peking and Hanoi too, but for your veteran anti-communist — especially back then — it is Russia which supplies the main focus of his venom.) A prominent editor of *National Review* once told me: "I have a vision, a great vision of the future: a totally devastated Soviet Union." I knew that it was this vision that really animated the new conservatism.

In response to all this, and seeing peace as the crucial political issue, a few friends and I became Stevensonian Democrats in 1960. I watched with increasing horror as the right wing, led by *National Review*, continually grew in strength and moved ever closer to real political power.

Having broken emotionally with the right wing, our tiny group of libertarians began to rethink many of our old, unexamined premises. First, we restudied the origins of the Cold War, we read our D.F. Fleming and we concluded, to our considerable surprise, that the United States was solely at fault in the Cold War, and that Russia was the aggrieved party. And this meant that the great danger to the peace and freedom of the world came not from Moscow or "international communism," but from the U.S. and its Empire stretching across and dominating the world.

And then we studied the foul European conservatism that had taken over the right wing; here we had statism in a virulent form, and yet no one could possibly think these conservatives to be "leftist." But this meant that our simple "left/total government — right/no government" continuum was altogether wrong and that our whole identification of ourselves as "extreme rightists" must contain a basic flaw. Plunging back into history, we again concentrated on the reality that in the nineteenth century, *laissez-faire* liberals and radicals were on the extreme left and our ancient foes, the conservatives, on the right. My old friend and libertarian colleague Leonard Liggio then came up with the following analysis of the historical process.

First there was the old order, the *ancien régime,* the regime of caste and frozen status, of exploitation by a despotic ruling class, using the church to dupe the masses into accepting its rule. This was pure statism; this was the right wing. Then, in seventeenth and eighteenth century western Europe, a liberal and radical opposition movement arose, our heroes, who championed a popular revolutionary movement on behalf of rationalism, individual liberty, minimal government, free markets, international peace and separation of church and state, in opposition to throne and altar, to monarchy, the ruling class, theocracy and war. These — "our people" — were the left, and the purer their vision the more "extreme" they were.

So far so good; but what of socialism, which we had always considered the extreme left? Where did that fit in? Liggio analyzed socialism as a confused middle-of-the-road movement, influenced historically by both the libertarian left and the conservative right. From the individualist left the socialists took the goals of freedom: the withering away of the state, the replacement of the governing of men by the administration of things, opposition to the ruling class and a search for its overthrow, the desire to establish international peace, an advanced industrial economy and a high standard of living for the mass of the people. From the right the socialists adopted the means to achieve these goals — collectivism, state planning, community control of the individual. This put socialism in the middle of the ideological spectrum. It also meant that socialism was an unstable, self-contradictory doctrine bound to fly apart in the inner contradiction between its means and ends.

Our analysis was greatly bolstered by our becoming familiar with the new and exciting group of historians who studied under University of Wisconsin historian William Appleman Williams. From them we discovered that all of us free marketeers had erred in believing that somehow, down deep, Big Businessmen were *really* in favor of *laissez-faire,* and that their deviations from it, obviously clear and notorious in recent years, were either "sellouts" of principle to expediency or the result of astute maneuverings by liberal intellectuals.

This is the general view on the right; in the remarkable phrase of Ayn Rand, Big Business is "America's most persecuted minority." Persecuted minority, indeed! Sure, there were thrusts against Big Business in the old McCormick *Chicago Tribune* and in the writings of Albert Jay Nock; but it took the Williams-[Gabriel] Kolko analysis to portray the true anatomy and physiology of the American scene.

As Kolko pointed out, all the various measures of federal regulation and welfare statism that left and right alike have always believed to be mass movements against Big Business are not only now backed to the hilt by Big Business, but were originated by it for the very purpose of shifting from a free market to a cartelized economy that would benefit it. Imperialistic foreign policy and the permanent garrison state originated in the Big Business drive for foreign investments and for war contracts at home.

The role of the liberal intellectuals is to serve as "corporate liberals," weavers of sophisticated apologias to inform the masses that the heads of the American corporate state are ruling on behalf of the "common good" and the "general welfare" — like the priest in the Oriental despotism who convinced the masses that their emperor was all-wise and divine.

Since the early 1960s, as the *National Review* right has moved nearer to political power, it has jettisoned its old libertarian remnants and has drawn ever closer to the liberals of the Great American Consensus. Evidence of this abounds. There is Bill Buckley's ever-widening popularity in the mass media and among liberal intellectuals, as well as widespread admiration on the intellectual right for people and groups it once despised:

for *The New Leader*, for Irving Kristol, for the late Felix Frankfurter (who always opposed judicial restraint on government invasions of individual liberty), for Hannah Arendt and Sidney Hook. Despite occasional bows to the free market, conservatives have come to agree that economic issues are unimportant; they therefore accept — or at least do not worry about — the major outlines of the Keynesian welfare-warfare state of liberal corporatism.

On the domestic front, virtually the only conservative interests are to suppress Negroes ("shoot looters," "crush those riots"), to call for more power for the police so as not to "shield the criminal" (i.e., not to protect his libertarian rights), to enforce prayer in the public schools, to put Reds and other subversives and "seditionists" in jail and to carry on the crusade for war abroad. There is little in the thrust of this program with which liberals can now disagree; any disagreements are tactical or matters of degree only. Even the Cold War — including the war in Vietnam — was begun and maintained and escalated by the liberals themselves.

No wonder that liberal Daniel Moynihan — a national board member of Americans for Democratic Action incensed at the radicalism of the current anti-war and Black Power movements—should recently call for a formal alliance between liberals and conservatives, since after all they basically agree on these, the two crucial issues of our time! Even Barry Goldwater has gotten the message; in January 1968 in *National Review*, Goldwater concluded an article by affirming that he is not against liberals, that liberals are needed as a counterweight to conservatism, and that he had in mind a fine liberal like Max Lerner — Max Lerner, the epitome of the old left, the hated symbol of my youth!

In response to our isolation from the right, and noting the promising signs of libertarian attitudes in the emerging new left, a tiny band of us ex-rightist libertarians founded the "little journal," *Left and Right*, in the spring of 1965. We had two major purposes: to make contact with libertarians already on the new left and to persuade the bulk of libertarians or quasi-libertarians who remained on the right to follow our example. We have been gratified in both directions: by the remarkable shift toward libertarian and anti-statist positions of the new left, and by the significant number of young people who have left the right-wing movement.

This left/right tendency has begun to be noticeable on the new left, praised and damned by those aware of the situation. (Our old colleague Ronald Hamowy, an historian at Stanford, set forth the left/right position in the *New Republic* collection, *Thoughts of the Young Radicals* [1966].)

We have received gratifying encouragement from Carl Oglesby who, in his *Containment and Change* (1967), advocated a coalition of new left and old right, and from the young scholars grouped around the unfortunately now defunct *Studies on the Left*. We've also been criticized, if indirectly, by Staughton Lynd, who worries because our ultimate goals — free market as against socialism — differ.

Finally, liberal historian Martin Duberman, in a recent issue of *Partisan Review*, sharply criticizes SNCC and CORE for being "anarchists," for rejecting the authority of the state, for insisting that community be voluntary, and for stressing, along with SDS, participatory instead of representative democracy. Perceptively, if on the wrong side of the fence, Duberman then links SNCC and the new left with us old rightists: "SNCC and CORE, like the Anarchists, talk increasingly of the supreme importance of the individual. They do so, paradoxically, in a rhetoric strongly reminiscent of that long associated with the right. It could be Herbert Hoover ... but it is in fact Rap Brown who now reiterates the Negro's need to stand on his own two feet, to make his own decisions, to develop self-reliance and a sense of self-worth. SNCC may be scornful of present-day liberals and 'statism,' but it seems hardly to realize that the *laissez-faire* rhetoric it prefers derives almost verbatim from the classic liberalism of John Stuart Mill." Tough. It could, I submit, do a lot worse.

I hope to have demonstrated why a few compatriots and I have shifted, or rather been shifted, from "extreme right" to "extreme left" in the past twenty years merely by staying in the same basic ideological place. The right wing, once in determined opposition to Big Government, has now become the conservative wing of the American corporate state and its foreign policy of expansionist imperialism. If we would salvage liberty from this deadening left/right fusion in the center, this needs be done through a counter-fusion of old right and new left.

James Burnham, an editor of *National Review* and its main strategic thinker in waging the "Third World War" (as he entitles his column), the prophet of the managerial state (in *The Managerial Revolution),* whose only hint of positive interest in liberty in a lifetime of political writing was a call for legalized firecrackers, recently attacked the dangerous trend among some young conservatives to make common cause with the left in opposing the draft. Burnham warned that he learned in his Trotskyite days that this would be an "unprincipled" coalition, and he warned that if one begins by being anti-draft one might wind up opposed to the war in Vietnam:

> And I rather think that some of them are at heart, or are getting to be, against the war. Murray Rothbard has shown how right-wing libertarianism can lead to almost as anti-US a position as left-wing libertarianism does. And a strain of isolationism has always been endemic in the American right.

This passage symbolizes how deeply the whole thrust of the right wing has changed in the last two decades. Vestigial interest in liberty or in opposition to war and imperialism are now considered deviations to be stamped out without delay. There are millions of Americans, I am convinced, who are still devoted to individual liberty and opposition to the Leviathan state at home and abroad, Americans who call themselves "conservatives" but feel that something has gone very wrong with the old anti-New Deal and anti-Fair Deal cause.

Something *has* gone wrong: the right wing has been captured and transformed by elitists and devotees of the European conservative ideals of order and militarism, by witch hunters and global crusaders, by statists who wish to coerce "morality" and suppress "sedition."

America was born in a revolution against Western imperialism, born as a haven of freedom against the tyrannies and despotism, the wars and intrigues of the old world. Yet we have allowed ourselves to sacrifice the American ideals of peace and freedom and anti-colonialism on the altar of a crusade to kill communists throughout the world; we have surrendered our libertarian birthright into the hands of those who yearn to restore the Golden Age of the Holy Inquisition. It is about time that we wake up and rise up to restore our heritage.

Index

abortion, 148
African-Americans, 37–38, 43–46, 102, 160
  and conscription, 122
  and conservatives, 159
  and Rothbard, 151
  as colonized people, 41–42, 46
Agnew, Spiro, 127–28
Algeria, 119
Americans for Democratic Action, 61, 62, 159
American Telephone and Telegraph, 50
Anarchism, 125–26, 160
An Austrian Perspective on the History of Economic Thought (Rothbard), 11
antiwar movement, 83–84, 100, 109–10, 129–30
  and liberalism, 159
Arendt, Hannah, 159

Bay of Pigs, 86
Biafra, 48
Boulding, Kenneth, 137
Bozell, L. Brent, 156
Britain, 69–70
Brown, H. Rap, 13, 46, 57, 160
Brundage, Avery, 96
Brezhnev, Leonid, 116
Bright, John, 152
Buckley, William F., Jr., 12, 147–48, 158–59
  as cold warrior, 154–55
Buffett, Howard, 152–53
Bukharin, Nicolai, 131
Bull of, Jack, 144–45
Burke, Edmund, 156
Burnham, James, 149, 155, 160–61
Business Executives Move for a Vietnam Peace, 55–56

Carmichael, Stokely, 46
Chambers, Whittaker, 155
Chamberlain, John, 155
Chicago Tribune, 152
  and Big Business, 158
  and Korean war, 153
China, 119, 126, 131–35
  and "Cultural Revolution," 132–34
Chodorov, Frank, 25, 152
Christian Economics, 12
Civil War (US), 48
Cobden, Richard, 152
Coffin, William Sloane, 84
Cohn-Bendit, Daniel, 125
collective security, 27–28
Columbia University, 111, 113–15
Commercial and Financial Chronicle, 152
Committee to Aid the National Liberation Front, 84

Communist Party, 126
China, 131–35
East Germany, 116
ex-communists, 155
France, 120
US, 153
Congress of Racial Equality, 160
conscription, 21–26, 31–34, 73–74, 104, 109, 121–22
and emigration, 110
and jury duty, 39–40
and libertarians, 148, 161
and Old Right, 151–52
The Conservative Mind (Kirk), 155
Conservative Union, 111
conservatism, 62, 63, 147–49
and draft, 160–61
and fascism, 149
and Lyndon Johnson, 62
and McCarthyism, 153–54
and *National Review*, 154–57
and Nixon, 148
and Old Right, 151–53
and statism, 148, 159
Containment and Change (Oglesby), 1160
Council for a Volunteer Military, 26
crime, 197–208
Cuba, 119
Cyprus, 69–70

Daley, Richard, 107
de Gaulle, Charles, 47, 67–68, 80, 115
de Maistre, Joseph, 156
de Toledano, Ralph, 155
Delury, John, 89–90
Democratic party, 66, 99
Dewey, Thomas E., 128
Dodd, Thomas J., 62
Douglas MacArthur Club, 111
draft, *see conscription*
Duberman, Martin, 160
Dutschke, Rudi, 116–17, 125

Eccles, Marriner S., 56
education, 15–16, 33–34, 83
and statism, 115–16
Eisenhower, Dwight, 56, 66
environmentalism, 137–45
Evers, Medgar, 117

Fair Deal, 123, 147, 161
Farmer, James, 26
fascism, 76, 83–84, 149
Fifield, James, 12
Fleming, D. F., 157
Flynn, John T., 152
Ford, Henry II, 50
France, 119–20
see also: de Gaulle, Charles
Frankfurter, Felix, 159
Freedom Newspapers, 12
Freedom School, 12
Friedenburg, Edgard Z., 34
Friedman, Milton, 26
Fulbright, William J., 105

Galenson, Walter, 132
Gandhi, Mahatma, 102
Garrison, William Lloyd, 149
Gavin, James M., 66
Garrison, Jim, 75–76
Gaza, 27
General Dynamics, 50
General Electric, 50
General Motors, 50
Germany, 126
Gimbel, Mike, 84
gold, 68, 79–82
Goldwater, Barry, 159
Gomulka, Wadislaw, 116
Goodman, Paul, 34
Greece, 69–70
Griswold v. Connecticut, 138
Grivas, Giorgio, 70
Guevara, Ernesto "Che," 116
Gulf of Tonkin, 86

Gullander, W. P., 50
gun control, 59–60

Halbrook, Stephen P., 131–35
Hamilton, Alexander, 156
Hamowy, Ronald, 159–60
Hatcher, Richard G., 66
Hatfield, Mark, 66
Herberg, Will, 155
Herbert, Auberon, 152
Hershey, Lewis B., 73, 84
Hess, Karl, 26
Hillenkoeter, Roscoe H., 153
Ho Chi Minh, 116
Hoiles, Raymond C., 12
homesteading, 148
Hook, Sidney, 159
Hoover, Herbert, 153, 160
Hoover, J. Edgar, 73, 125
Hughes, Richard J., 43, 65
Humphrey, Charles, 74
Humphrey, Hubert, 103, 112, 123, 128
    and civil liberties, 154
Hungarian Revolution (1956), 119

Industrial Revolution, 140
Israel, 28, 35–36

Japan, 126
Jackson, Andrew, 149
Jackson, Henry M., 86
Jefferson, Thomas, 149, 152, 156
Johnson, Lyndon, 13, 45–46, 50, 61–62, 65–66, 71, 80, 81–82, 93–94
    and Eugene McCarthy, 111–12
    and peace talks, 105–06
    withdraws, 99–100, 103
Jones, LeRoi, 84

Katanga, 48
Kempton, Murray, 86
Kendall, Willmoore, 156
Kennedy, John F., 101, 117
Kennedy, Joseph P., 153
Kennedy, Robert F., 103, 105, 117
Kerr, Clark, 13, 15
Keynes, John Maynard, 51, 52, 82, 152
Keynesianism, *see Keynes, John Maynard*
King, Martin Luther, 13, 99, 101–02, 107, 117
Kirk, Grayson, 113–14
Kirk, Russell, 155
Kolko, Gabriel, 49, 158
Korean war, 56, 106, 153, 154
Kristol, Irving, 159

Lamont, Corliss, 153
Lefevre, Robert, 12
Left and Right, 12, 159
Lerner, Max, 159
Liggio, Leonard, 12, 157–58
liberalism, 46, 50, 61–62
    and Old Right, 147
    corporate, 158
    of Eugene McCarthy, 112
libertarian movement, 26, 49
    and New Left, 135, 159–60
    and Nixon, 123–24
    "left"-libertarians, 13–14
    split with conservatives, 147–49, 157–58
Lindsay, John, 89–90, 107
Liu Shao-chi, 132–33, 135
Lynd, Staughton, 160
Lyons, Eugene, 155

Madison, James, 156
Malthus, Thomas, 140
The Managerial Revolution (Burnham), 160
Mao Tse-tung, 116, 131–35
Malcolm X, 117
Man, Economy, and State (Rothbard), 11
Matthews, J. B., 155

McCarran Act, 154
McCarthy, Eugene, 66, 103, 105–06, 112, 123
McCarthy, Joseph, 153–54
McNamara, Robert S., 22
Mencken, Henry L., 147, 156
Metternich, Klemens von, 156
Meyer, Frank S., 155
Mill, John Stuart, 160
Morton, Thruston, 56, 66
Moynihan, Daniel Patrick, 159

The Nation, 152
  and red-baiting, 153
National Association of Manufacturers, 50
National Liberation Front of Vietnam, 56, 71–72, 87–88, 91–94, 106, 112
  program of, 97–98
National Review, 147–49, 154–57, 160
  and liberalism, 158–59
  and Rothbard, 12
nationalism, 48
NATO, 152
New Deal, 29, 49, 123, 161
  and Old Right, 147
The New Leader, 159
New Left, 15–16, 50, 120, 122
  and Rothbard, 13–14, 151, 158–60
The New Republic, 153
Niles, Henry E., 56
Nineteen Eighty-Four (Orwell), 76
Ninth Amendment, 138
Nixon, Richard, 13, 103, 123–24, 127–28
  and conservatives, 148
Nock, Albert J., 147, 156, 158
Nunn, Louie B., 65

Oglesby, Carl, 160
O'Hara, Almerin, C., 43–44
Old Right, 12, 151–53
  and Robert Taft, 130
Olympics, 95–96
Oswald in New Orleans (Weisberg), 76

pacifism, 107
Paine, Thomas, 149, 152, 156
Partisan Review, 160
Peace and Freedom Party, 151
Percy, Charles, 66
police brutality, 119–20
Power and Market (Rothbard), 11
Progressive movement, 49
Prohibition, 59–60

Quebec, 47–48

Rand, Ayn, 14, 49, 158
Ratliff, John Milton, 73–74
Reagan, Ronald, 13, 16
Republican party, 65–66, 127–30
  and McCarthyism, 154
  and Old Right, 152
Rockefeller, David, 50
Rockefeller, Nelson, 90, 103, 123
Romney, George W., 66, 103
Roosevelt, Franklin, 61, 62
  and civil liberties, 154
Rostow, Walter, 112
Rothbard, Murray N., 11–14
  and Old Right, 151–53
  and *National Review*, 156–57
  and New Left, 151, 158–60
Rueff, Jacques, 68, 80
Ruml, Beardsley, 54
Rusk, Dean, 77
Russia, 126, 134–35

Savio, Mario, 13, 15
Schlamm, William S., 155
Schlesinger, Arthur, Jr., 155
secession, 47–48
socialism
  as centrism, 157–58
  in Israel, 35–36
  on war, 55

Socrates, 156
Spanish-American War, 94
Spencer, Herbert, 152
Spiritual Mobilization, 12
Spock, Benjamin, 84
Spooner, Lysander, 152
Stalin, Joseph, 61, 131
Stassen, Harold, 129
Stokes, Carl, 66
"Strategy for Libertarian Social Change" (Rothbard), 11
Student Nonviolent Coordinating Committee, 46, 57, 160
Students for a Democratic Society, 74, 160
Studies on the Left, 160
Sulzberger, C. L., 125

Taft, Robert A., 130, 147, 149, 152
taxes, 49–52, 148
  withholding, 53–54
Taylor Law, 89
Teague, Walter, 84
Thomas, Norman, 26
Thoreau, Henry David, 152, 156
Thoughts of the Young Radicals (Kopind), 160
Thurmond, Strom, 86
Trotsky, Leon, 131
Trotskyists, 134, 160
True, Arnold, 56
Truman, David, 113–14
Truman, Harry, 61, 62
Truman Doctrine, 152–53
Tucker, Benjamin R., 152
Turkey, 69–70

U-2 incident, 86
United Nations, 28, 153

Vietcong, *see National Liberation Front of Vietnam*
Vietnam war, 13, 43, 44, 45, 55–56, 65, 66, 71–72, 77–78, 85–88, 91–92, 99–100, 109–10, 119
  and Eugene McCarthy, 111–12
  and liberals, 159
  and National Liberation Front, 97–98
  and peace talks, 105–06
  and Rothbard, 159
The Vigil (Rothbard), 12
Village Voice, 109

Walter, Paul W., Jr., 129–30
Warren Commission, 76
Weisberg, Harold, 76
Westmoreland, William, 92
Wheelwright, E. L., 132
Williams, William Appleman, 158
Wilson, James Harold, 79, 82
Wirtz, Willard, 22
Wittfogel, Karl, 155
World War I, 94
World War II, 94
Wrong, Dennis H., 141

Young Americans for Freedom, 109–10

Zionism, 36
zoning laws, 17

Made in the USA
Monee, IL
08 November 2026

67377465R00096